Divorce
in Kansas

*The Legal Process,
Your Rights and What to Expect*

Scott M. Mann, Esq.
Stephanie Tucker Muir, Esq.

Addicus Books
Omaha, Nebraska

Typography by Jack Kusler

This book is not intended to serve as a substitute for an attorney. Nor is it the author's intent to give legal advice contrary to that of an attorney.

Library of Congress Cataloging-in-Publication Data

Names: Mann, Scott M., —author. | Muir, Stephanie Tucker, —author.
Title: Divorce in Kansas : the legal process, your rights, and what to expect / Scott M. Mann, Stephanie Tucker Muir.
Description: Omaha, Nebraska : Addicus Books, 2017. | Series: Divorce in | Includes bibliographical references and index.
Identifiers: LCCN 2016042016 (print) | LCCN 2016042985 (ebook) | ISBN 9781943886319 (paperback) | ISBN 9781943886623 (PDF)| ISBN 9781943886647 (MOBI) | ISBN 9781943886630 (EPUB)
Subjects: LCSH: Divorce—Law and legislation—Kansas. | Divorce suits—Kansas. | Equitable distribution of marital property—Kansas. | Custody of children—Kansas. | BISAC: LAW / Family Law / Divorce & Separation. | FAMILY & RELATIONSHIPS / Divorce & Separation.
Classification: LCC KFK100 .M36 2017 (print) | LCC KFK100 (ebook) | DDC 346.78101/66—dc23
LC record available at https://lccn.loc.gov/2016042016

Addicus Books, Inc.
P.O. Box 45327
Omaha, Nebraska 68145
www.AddicusBooks.com
Printed in the United States of America
10 9 8 7 6 5 4 3 2 1

To our clients past and present. Their courage and generosity of spirit continues to inspire and teach us each day.

Contents

Acknowledgements

Few authors publish without the hard work and assistance of many others and this book is no exception. Our first acknowledgment goes to the past and present clients of MannTuckerMuir, LLC, The Family Law Firm. Each day they trust us to guide them through a confusing and uncertain time of their lives. They are willing to be courageous, truthful, and vulnerable, teaching us what goes on in the minds and hearts of people experiencing divorce. We are so grateful for their sacred trust. They inspire us to continue to strive for excellence.

We thank our publisher, Rod Colvin of Addicus Books, for the opportunity to write this book. His support made it possible for our work to benefit people all across Kansas.

Members of the family law bench and bar in Kansas have contributed more to this book than they realize. Their depth of knowledge and commitment to excellence both taught and inspired us.

Our team at MannTuckerMuir, LLC is wholly dedicated to making the process of divorce easier for our clients, constantly searching for the best practices to support our clients and make the process easier for them. Much of what you see in this book is due to their committed work over the years.

Our families have also inspired and encouraged us in this project. We are each very blessed to have their enduring support.

Finally, we greatly appreciate the assistance of our paralegal, Kayte Charlesworth, in the completion of this project.

If this book empowers readers on their divorce journey as we hope, it is only because of the generosity of so many, for which we extend our heartfelt gratitude.

Introduction

Nearly every day we meet with men and women who are struggling in their everyday lives as they contemplate and move through divorce. Whether you initiate or respond to a divorce, you are facing a change in every single part of your life. No area remains untouched from a divorce action. Parenting, family relationships, finances, social networks, personal belongings, a residence, job performance—all effect how your entire personal world is altered in divorce. Our purpose in writing *Divorce in Kansas* was to help you navigate through an uncertain journey.

Divorce is hard. We see our courageous clients, like you, making tough decisions every day in the face of their changing worlds. We know from our own experience and in counseling hundreds of clients over the years, that in order to reach a place of growth and healing, it requires a tremendous amount of support throughout the journey. *Divorce in Kansas* was written to be a part of helping you move through this time of transition with more clarity and ease. It is not intended to be a substitute for advice from your lawyer. Rather, it is designed to assist you in partnering with your lawyer to reach your goals in the resolution of your divorce.

In writing *Divorce in Kansas,* we endeavor to partner with you and explain each step in the hope that it will lead to your empowerment. The more control and clarity you feel over the process, the better you are able to make sound decisions regarding very challenging choices. We hope you will use this book as a guide to ask your lawyer questions, to understand what it is you are unclear about, and to begin seeing the big picture of the journey upon which you are about to embark.

We hope this book will be used not only by people going through divorce, but also by professionals who support you—attorneys, mediators, therapists, clergy, financial advisors, coaches, and others who are called upon to serve people who are divorcing. Although every divorce is different and your circumstances unique, we hope that *Divorce in Kansas* will begin to answer your multitude of questions as you begin this brave road toward a new beginning.

During your divorce, you will have hard, grief-filled days and you will face mountains of uncertainty, but you will get through this. We promise you. In the end, you will inevitably find some relief in the letting go of old sadness, glimmers of hope in recreating yourself, and a sure sense of new possibilities for your future.

1

Understanding the Divorce Process

At a time when your life can feel like it's in utter chaos, sometimes the smallest bit of predictability can bring a sense of comfort. The outcome of many aspects of your divorce may be unknown, increasing your fear and anxiety. But there is one part of your divorce that does have some measure of predictability and that is the divorce process itself.

Most divorces proceed in a step-by-step manner. Despite the uniqueness of your divorce, you can generally count on one phase of your divorce following the next. Sometimes just realizing you are completing stages and moving forward with your divorce can reassure you that it won't go on forever.

Develop a basic understanding of the divorce process. This will lower your anxiety when your attorney starts talking about "depositions" or "going to trial", and you feel your heart start pounding in fear. It can reduce your frustration about the length of the process because you understand why each step is needed. It will support you to begin preparing for what comes next. Most importantly, understanding the divorce process will make your experience of the entire divorce easier. Who wouldn't prefer that?

1.1   What is my first step?

Find a law firm that handles divorces as a regular part of its law practice. The best recommendations come from people who have knowledge of a lawyer's experience and reputation.

Even if you are not ready to file for divorce, call to schedule an appointment right away to obtain information about protecting yourself and your children. Even if you are not planning to file for divorce, your spouse might be.

Ask what documents you should take to your initial consultation. Make a list of your questions to bring to your first meeting. Start making plans for how you will pay your attorney to begin work on your case.

1.2   Must I have an attorney to get a divorce in Kansas?

You are not required to have an attorney to obtain a divorce in Kansas. However, if your case involves minor children, alimony or spousal support, significant property or assets, or debts, you should avoid proceeding on your own.

If your divorce does not involve any of these issues, call your local courthouse to see whether there is a self-help desk available to provide assistance. A person who proceeds in a legal matter without a lawyer is referred to as being *pro se,* on one's own.

If you are considering proceeding without an attorney, at a minimum have an initial consultation with an attorney to discuss your rights and duties under the law. You may have certain rights or obligations you are unaware of. Meeting with a lawyer can help you decide whether to proceed on your own.

1.3   What are the steps taken in a divorce action?

The divorce process in Kansas typically involves the following steps.

If you are initiating the divorce:

- Obtain a referral for a lawyer.
- Schedule an appointment with an attorney.
- Prepare questions and gather necessary documents for an initial consultation.
- Meet for an initial consultation with an attorney.
- Pay the attorney a fee deposit and sign a representation agreement.
- Provide requested information and documents to your attorney.
- Take other actions as advised by your attorney, such as opening or closing financial accounts.

- Attorney prepares the summons and petition for divorce, and any other necessary initial paperwork, for your review and signature.
- Attorney files the summons and petition with the clerk of the court. You would be referred to in all court papers as the *petitioner.*
- Attorney serves the summons and petition on the *respondent,* your spouse.
- If interim relief (such as temporary child support, spousal support, or attorney fees) is appropriate, attorney prepares motion papers for your review and signature, files with the court, obtains court date, and serves pleadings on your spouse.

If you have been served with divorce papers:

- Obtain a referral for a lawyer.
- Schedule an appointment with an attorney.
- Prepare questions and gather necessary documents for an initial consultation.
- Meet for an initial consultation with an attorney.
- Pay the attorney a fee deposit and sign a representation agreement.
- Provide requested information and documents to your attorney.
- Take other actions as advised by your attorney, such as opening or closing financial accounts.
- Attorney prepares a response, the "answer", to the summons and petition for your review and signature.
- Attorney files your response with the clerk of the court within thirty days of service of the petition and summons on you.
- If you are served with requests for interim relief, attorney prepares your response to these moving papers.

After an action has been commenced and the response filed:

- With the assistance of your attorney, you need to prepare financial disclosure documents (income and expense declaration and preliminary schedule of assets and debts). In Kansas this financial disclosure is called a *domestic relations affidavit* or a *DRA.*

- Negotiations begin regarding temporary custody and visitation, child and spousal support, payment of community obligations, and attorney fees.
- Attorney prepares moving papers for any requests for temporary relief not previously made.
- If there are minor children, the parties comply with any local rules or court orders to attend parent orientation class and to participate in mandatory mediation.
- Court holds hearing(s) held on requests for temporary relief.
- Either the parties reach an agreement or the court issues temporary orders.
- Temporary order is prepared by one attorney, approved as to form by other attorney, and submitted to the judge for signature.
- Both sides conduct *discovery*—the process designed to obtain information regarding all relevant facts, and commence the process to exchange valuations of all assets, including expert opinions if needed.
- You confer with your attorney to review facts, identify issues, assess strengths and weaknesses of case, review strategy, and develop a settlement proposal.
- Spouses, with the support of their attorneys, attempt to reach agreement through written proposals, mediation, settlement conferences, or other forms of negotiation.

If you reach an agreement on all issues, then:

- One attorney prepares marital settlement agreement and necessary judgment paperwork. These drafts are reviewed by the other attorney and by both spouses.
- Both parties sign the agreement and all necessary paperwork.
- Judgment paperwork is signed by the attorneys and filed with the court.
- Either the parties waive the court date or the court holds a brief, final hearing.

- Judgment is entered and you will be divorced.
- Your attorney completes necessary orders and supervises the property transfer until all agreed-upon terms are satisfied.

If you are unable to reach an agreement on all issues, then:

- Your attorney completes all necessary discovery to bring the case to its trial-ready point.
- Your attorney obtains a trial date.
- If agreement has been reached on any issues, your attorney prepares a stipulation on those issues. All other issues are set for trial.
- You work with your attorney to prepare your case for trial.
- Your attorney prepares witnesses, trial exhibits, legal research on contested issues, pretrial motions, trial briefs, direct and cross-examination of witnesses, opening statements, witness subpoenas, and your closing argument.
- You meet with your attorney for final trial preparation.
- Trial is held.
- The judge may make decisions at the conclusion of the trial, or more often will take the matter under advisement and will issue a decision several weeks later.
- The judge issues a statement of decision or directs the statement to be prepared by one attorney.
- The other attorney may make any objections they have to the statement of decision. If appropriate, the court sets the matter for hearing to resolve any objections.
- The judge signs the decree of divorce dissolving your marriage.
- The attorneys supervise any property transfers until all agreed-upon terms are satisfied.

Your posttrial rights are discussed in the section on appeals.

1.4 Is Kansas a *no-fault state* or do I need grounds for a divorce?

Kansas, like most states, is a *no-fault divorce state*. This means that neither you nor your spouse is required to prove that the other is "at fault" in order to be granted a divorce. Factors such as infidelity, cruelty, or abandonment are not necessary to receive a divorce in Kansas, although they do still exist as grounds for a divorce. Rather, in most cases it is necessary only to prove the "no-fault" grounds the parties are no longer compatible, or that they are "incompatible," to have the marriage dissolved.

Although not generally required, if either party chooses to have a final hearing, then the testimony of either you or your spouse is likely to be sufficient evidence for the court to rule that the marriage should be dissolved and the divorce granted. This testimony will state what efforts at reconciliation were made, if any, that those efforts were not successful, that further attempts would not be beneficial, and that the parties are "incompatible."

Most settled cases are finalized without a final hearing or court appearance before a judge. If a trial is necessary or a trial hearing is held, the judge may ask for information regarding the nature of the problems that led to the divorce or the type of reconciliation efforts made, such as counseling with a therapist or clergy member.

1.5 How will a judge view infidelity or my spouse's infidelity?

Because Kansas is a no-fault divorce state, there will rarely be testimony or evidence introduced about either spouse's infidelity. However, the judge may allow testimony regarding an extramarital affair if custody is an issue and your child was exposed to the affair.

1.6 Do I have to get divorced in the same state I married in?

No. Regardless of where you were married, you may seek a divorce in Kansas if the jurisdictional requirements of residency are met. The jurisdictional requirements are discussed in the following question.

1.7 How long must I have lived in Kansas to get a divorce in the state?

Either you or your spouse must have been a resident of Kansas for at least sixty days prior to the date your divorce case is filed with the court to meet the *residency requirement* for a divorce in Kansas.

If neither party meets the residency requirement and there is an extraordinary situation or emergency circumstance, there may be other legal options available for your protection. If you do not meet the sixty-day residency requirement, talk to your attorney about options such as a protection order.

1.8 My spouse has told me she will never "give" me a divorce. Can I get one in Kansas anyway?

Yes. Kansas does not require that your spouse agree to a divorce. If your spouse threatens to not "give" you a divorce, know that in Kansas this is likely to be an idle threat without any basis in the law.

Under Kansas law, to obtain a divorce you must be able to prove that you and your spouse are "incompatible." This is a legal term meaning that one sees no possibility of reconciliation between you or your spouse. In short, it is not necessary to have your spouse agree to the divorce or to allege the specific difficulties that arose during the marriage to obtain a divorce in Kansas.

1.9 Can I divorce my spouse in Kansas if he or she lives in another state?

Provided you have met the residency requirements for living in Kansas for sixty days, you can file for divorce here even if your spouse lives in another state.

Discuss with your attorney the facts that will need to be proven and the steps necessary to give your spouse proper notice to ensure that the court will have jurisdiction over your spouse. Your attorney can counsel you on whether it is possible to proceed with the divorce.

1.10 Can I get a divorce even when I don't know where my spouse is currently living?

Kansas law allows you to proceed with a divorce even if you do not know the current address of your spouse. First, take action to attempt to locate your spouse. Contact family members, friends, former coworkers, or anyone else who might know your spouse's whereabouts. Utilize resources on the Internet that are designed to help locate people.

Let your attorney know of the efforts you have made to attempt to find your spouse. Inform your lawyer of your spouse's last known address, as well as any work address or other address where this person may be found. Once your attorney attempts to give notice to your spouse without success, it is possible to ask the court to proceed with the divorce by giving notice through publication in a newspaper.

Although your divorce may be granted following service of notice by publication in a newspaper, you may not be able to get other court orders such as those for child support or alimony without giving personal notice to your spouse. Talk to your attorney about your options and rights if you don't know where your spouse is living.

1.11 I just moved to a different county within the state of Kansas. Do I have to file in the county where my spouse lives?

You may file your divorce complaint either in the county where you reside or in the county where your spouse resides.

1.12 I immigrated to Kansas. Will my immigration status stop me from getting a divorce?

If you meet the residency requirements for divorce in Kansas, you can get a divorce here regardless of your immigration status. Talk to your immigration lawyer about the likelihood of a divorce leading to immigration challenges.

If you are a victim of domestic violence, tell your lawyer. You may be eligible for a change in your immigration status under the federal *Violence Against Women Act*.

1.13 I want to get divorced in my Indian tribal court. What do I need to know?

Each tribal court has its own laws governing divorce. Requirements for residency, grounds for divorce, and the laws regarding property, alimony, and children can vary substantially from state law. Some tribes have very different laws governing the grounds for your divorce, removal of children from the home, and cohabitation.

Contact an attorney who is knowledgeable about the law in your tribal court for legal advice on pursuing a divorce in your tribal court or on the requirements for recording a divorce obtained in state court with the clerk of the tribal court.

1.14 Is there a waiting period for a divorce in Kansas?

Yes. Kansas has a mandatory sixty-day waiting period. This waiting period begins on the day that the petition for divorce is filed with the court. However, the *respondent,* the person who did not initiate the divorce process, must also be provided with legal notice of the divorce. This date is either the day that the respondent is personally served or delivered papers by the sheriff, or the date that the respondent files with the court a "voluntary appearance" acknowledging that he or she knows the divorce has been filed with the court.

If you did not initiate the divorce filing with the court and you are the respondent, you will typically have twenty-eight days to file a written response, or "answer," to the divorce petition (discussed further below) your spouse filed. Even with the longer sixty-day waiting period, if you fail to file an answer to the petition within the deadline to answer, you may be considered in "default" and the court may proceed to resolve the case without any further notice to or input from you. Confer with your attorney if you have any concerns about the answer deadline.

1.15 What is a *divorce petition?*

A *petition for divorce* is a document signed by the person filing for divorce and filed with the clerk of the court to initiate the divorce process. The petition will set forth in very general terms what the petitioner is asking the court to order. (See a sample petition for divorce in the Appendix.)

1.16 My spouse said she filed for divorce last week, but my lawyer says there's nothing on file at the courthouse. What does it mean to "file for divorce?"

When lawyers use the term "filing" they are ordinarily referring to filing a legal document at the courthouse, such as delivering a petition for divorce to the clerk of the court. Sometimes a person who has hired a lawyer to begin a divorce action uses the phrase "I've filed for divorce," although no papers have yet been taken to the courthouse to start the legal process. Today in most Kansas counties, the courts require electronic filing of all court papers, so divorce papers are rarely taken to the courthouse.

1.17 If we both want a divorce, does it matter who files?

No. In the eyes of the court, the *petitioner* (the party who files the petition initiating the divorce process) and the *respondent* (the other spouse) are not seen differently by virtue of which party filed. The court, as a neutral decision maker, will not give preference to either party. Both parties will be given adequate notice and each will have a chance to be heard and present argument.

1.18 Are there advantages to filing first?

It depends. Discuss with your attorney whether there are any advantages to you filing first. Your attorney may advise you to file first or to wait until your spouse files, depending upon the overall strategy for your case and your circumstances. For example, if there is a concern that your spouse will begin to transfer assets upon learning about your plans for divorce, your attorney might advise you to seek a temporary restraining order to protect against such an action, without giving prior notice to your spouse. However, if you are separated from your spouse but have a beneficial temporary arrangement, your attorney may counsel you to wait for your spouse to file.

Allow your attorney to support you in making the decision about whether and when to initiate the legal process by filing a petition for divorce.

1.19 Can I stop the newspaper from publishing notice of the filing or granting of my divorce?

Documents filed with the court, such as a divorce petition or a final decree are matters of public record. Newspapers have a right to access this information, and some local newspapers publish this information as a matter of routine. There is no set schedule to determine when this information will be published. Contact your local newspaper to learn more.

In rare cases, a divorce file may be kept private, referred to as being "sealed" or "under seal" if the court orders it.

1.20 Is there a way to avoid embarrassing my spouse and not have the sheriff serve him with the divorce papers at his workplace?

Yes. Talk to your lawyer about the option of having your spouse sign a document known as a *voluntary entry of appearance*. The signing and filing of this document with the court can eliminate the need to have your spouse served by the sheriff. (See a sample in the Appendix.)

The use of a voluntary entry of appearance is not appropriate for all cases, so discuss with your attorney the better choice for your case.

1.21 Should I sign a voluntary appearance even if I don't agree with what my spouse has written in the complaint for divorce?

Signing the voluntary appearance does not mean that you agree with anything your spouse has stated in the divorce complaint or anything that your spouse is asking for in the divorce.

Signing the voluntary appearance only substitutes for having the sheriff personally hand you the documents. You do not waive the right to object to anything your spouse has stated in the complaint for dissolution of marriage.

Follow your attorney's advice on whether and when to sign a voluntary appearance.

1.22 Why should I contact an attorney right away if I have received divorce papers?

If your spouse has filed for divorce, it is important that you obtain legal advice as soon as possible. Even if you and your spouse are getting along, having independent legal counsel can help you make decisions now that could affect your divorce later.

After your spouse has filed for divorce, a temporary hearing can be scheduled at any time. It is possible you will receive only a few days' notice of a temporary hearing. You will be better prepared for a temporary hearing if you have already retained an attorney.

After your voluntary appearance has been filed with the court or you have been served by the sheriff, a written answer responding to your spouse's divorce complaint must be filed with the court within twenty to thirty days, depending upon the facts in your case.

1.23   What is an *ex parte court order?*

An *ex parte court order* is obtained by one party going to the judge to ask for something without giving prior notice or an opportunity to be heard by the other side.

With the exception of restraining orders, judges are reluctant to sign *ex parte* orders. Ordinarily the court will require the other side to have notice of any requests for court orders, and a hearing before the judge will be held.

An *affidavit,* which is a written statement sworn under oath, is usually required before a judge will sign an *ex parte* order. *Ex parte* orders are generally limited to emergency situations, such as requests for temporary restraining orders and protection orders.

When an *ex parte* order is granted, the party who did not request the order will have an opportunity to have a subsequent hearing before the judge to determine whether the order should remain in effect.

1.24   What is a *motion?*

A *motion* is a request that the judge enter a court order of some type. For example, your attorney may file a written motion with the court asking for an order related to temporary child custody, child support, parenting time, or financial matters, such as payment of bills.

Some motions are made to handle certain procedural aspects of your case, such as a motion for a continuance asking that a court date be changed or a motion for extension of time asking that the court extend a deadline. In some cases a motion may be made orally rather than in writing, for example when an issue arises during the course of a court hearing or trial.

1.25   Once my petition for divorce is filed, how soon can a temporary hearing be held to decide what happens with our child and our finances while the divorce is pending?

In most cases a temporary hearing can be held within sixty days of your divorce being filed with the court, assuming your spouse can be located to be given notice.

1.26   How much notice will I get if my spouse seeks a temporary order?

Kansas law requires that you receive reasonable notice of any court hearings. In the case of motions for temporary orders, this notice may be as short as seven days.

1.27   During my divorce, what am I responsible for doing?

Your attorney will explain what actions you should take to further the divorce process and to help you reach the best possible outcome.

You will be asked to:

- Keep in regular contact with your attorney.
- Update your attorney regarding any changes in your contact information, such as address, phone numbers, and e-mail address.
- Provide your attorney with all requested documents.
- Provide requested information in a timely manner.
- Complete forms and questionnaires.
- Appear in court on time.
- Be direct about asking any questions you might have.
- Tell your attorney your thoughts on settlement or what you would like the judge to order in your case.
- Remain respectful toward your spouse throughout the process.
- Keep your children out of the litigation.

- Comply with any temporary court orders, such as restraining or support orders.
- Advise your attorney of any significant developments in your case.

By doing your part in the divorce process, you enable your attorney to partner with you for a better outcome while also lowering your attorney fees.

1.28   I'm worried that I won't remember to ask my lawyer about all of the issues in my case. How can I be sure I don't miss anything?

Write down all of the topics you want to discuss with your attorney, including what your goals are for the outcome of the divorce. The sooner you clarify your goals, the easier it will be for your attorney to help you to get what you want. Realize that your attorney will think of some issues that you may not be thinking of. Your lawyer's experience will be helpful in making sure nothing important is forgotten.

Divorce Issues Checklist

Issue	Notes
Divorce	
Custody of minor children	
Removal of children from jurisdiction	
Parenting plan	
Child support	
Deviation from child-support guidelines	
Abatement of child support	
Travel expenses to facilitate parenting time for out-of-town/state parents	
Life insurance to fund unpaid child support	
Automatic withholding for support	
Child support arrearage from temporary order	
Child-care expenses	
Child-care credit	

Divorce Issues Checklist (Continued)

Issue	Notes
Heath insurance on minor children	
Uninsured medical expenses for minor children	
Qualified medical support order	
Private school tuition for children	
College expenses for children	
College savings accounts for the benefit of children	Matt pay for Will & Laurel Business or school
Health insurance on the parties	mine FCF?
Real property: rentals, cabins, commercial property	
Time-shares	
Retirement accounts	I need more than him
Federal or military pensions	
Business interests	Can I own part of FCF
Bank accounts	
Investments	I need more 60/40
Stock options	
Stock purchase plans	
Life insurance policies	Can I have some of this
Frequent flyer miles	
Credit card points	
Season tickets for events	
Premarital or nonmarital assets	My inhert not part of plan
Premarital or nonmarital debts	
Pets	
Personal property division: including motor vehicles, recreational vehicles, campers, airplanes, collections, furniture, electronics, tools, and household goods	He gets the crap

15

Divorce Issues Checklist (Continued)

Issue	Notes
Exchange date for personal property	
Division of marital debt	House, Subaru ???
Property settlement	
Alimony or spousal support (maintenance)	I need more
Life insurance to fund unpaid alimony	
Arrearage of alimony from temporary order	
Tax exemption for minor children	
IRS Form 8332	
Filing status for tax returns for last/current year	
Former name restoration	yes
Attorney fees	He pays

1.29 My spouse has all of our financial information. How will I be able to prepare for negotiations and trial if I don't know the facts or have the documents?

Once your divorce has been filed with court and temporary matters have been addressed, your attorney will proceed with a process known as *discovery.*

Through discovery, your attorney can ask your spouse to provide documents and information needed to prepare your case. Your attorney can also subpoena information directly from an institution—like a bank—to obtain the requested documentation.

1.30 My spouse and I both want our divorce to be amicable. How can we keep it that way?

You and your spouse are to be acknowledged for your willingness to cooperate while focusing on moving through the divorce process. This will not only make your lives easier and save you money on attorney fees, but it is also more likely to result in an outcome you are both satisfied with.

Find a lawyer who understands your goal to reach settlement and encourage your spouse to do the same.

16

Cooperate with the prompt exchange of necessary information. Then ask your attorney about the options of mediation and negotiation for reaching agreement. Even if you are not able to settle all of the issues in your divorce, these actions can increase the likelihood of agreement on many of the terms of your divorce decree.

1.31   Can I pick my judge?

You may not pick your own judge. "Judge shopping" occurs when a person involved in a legal case attempts to influence the court's assignment of a case so that it will be directed to or away from a particular judge. However, talk to your attorney about the reasons you want a different judge. If you believe that your judge has a conflict of interest, such as being a close friend of your spouse, you may have a basis for asking the judge to be "recused" in order to allow another judge to hear the case.

1.32   How long will it take to get my divorce?

The more you and your spouse are in agreement, the faster your divorce will conclude. At a minimum, there will usually be a sixty-day wait from the date the petition is filed with the court. In very rare instances, where there is an actual emergency circumstance, the court can waive the sixty-day waiting period requirement.

Assuming all issues, such as custody, support, property, and debts, are completely settled between you and your spouse, if you so choose or the court requires, a final hearing can be held any time after the sixty-day waiting period. Otherwise, your decree can be submitted to the judge for his or her approval any time after the sixty-day waiting period. Most people choose not to have a final hearing when they have reached an agreement on all of their issues.

If you and your spouse cannot agree on all of your issues and a trial to the judge is necessary, it can take six months to a year or even longer before your case may be concluded and a divorce decree or order entered by the court. However, your divorce will still not be "final" for all purposes, as either party may pursue an appeal or file posttrial motions.

1.33   What is the significance of my divorce being final?

The finality of your decree of divorce is important for many reasons. It can affect your right to remarry, your eligibility for health insurance from your former spouse, your filing status for income taxes, and your right to appeal the judge's decisions.

1.34   When does my divorce become final?

Your divorce becomes final for different purposes on different dates. The date that triggers the time period for a divorce becoming final is the date that the divorce decree is entered by court. In most cases, this will be the day the judge signs your divorce decree and the clerk files, or enters, it in your court file or the next business day.

Your divorce is final thirty days from the date it is entered by the court unless an appeal or a posttrial motion is filed.

1.35   Can I start using my former name right away and how do I get my name legally restored?

You may begin using your former name at any time, provided you are not doing so for any unlawful purpose, such as to avoid your creditors. Many agencies and institutions, however, will not alter their records without a court order changing your name.

If you want your former name restored, let your attorney know so that this provision can be included in your divorce decree.

2

Coping with Stress
during the Divorce Process

It may have been a few years ago. Or, it may have been many years ago. Perhaps it was only months. But, when you said, "I do," you meant it. Like most people getting married, you planned to be a happily married couple for life.

But things happen. Life brings change. People change. Whatever the circumstance, you now find yourself considering divorce. The emotions of divorce run from one extreme to another as you journey through the process. You may feel relief and ready to move on with your life. On the other hand, you may feel emotions that are quite painful. Anger. Fear. Sorrow. A deep sense of loss or failure. Remember, it is important to find support for coping with all these strong emotions.

Because going through a divorce can be an emotional time, having a clear understanding of the divorce process and what to expect will help you make better decisions. And, when it comes to decision making, search inside yourself to clarify your intentions and goals for the future. Let these intentions be your guide.

2.1   My spouse left home weeks ago. I don't want a divorce because I feel our marriage can be saved. Should I still see an attorney?

It's a good idea to see an attorney. Whether you want a divorce or not, there may be important actions for you to take now to protect your assets, credit, home, children, and future right to support.

If your spouse files for divorce, a temporary hearing could be heard in just a matter of days. It is best to be prepared with the support of an attorney, even if you decide not to file for a divorce at this time.

2.2 The thought of going to a lawyer's office to talk about divorce is more than I can bear. I canceled the first appointment I made because I just couldn't do it. What should I do?

Many people going through a divorce are dealing with lawyers for the first time and feel anxious about the experience. Ask a trusted friend or family member to go with you. He or she can support you by writing down your questions in advance, by taking notes for you during the meeting, and by helping you to remember what the lawyer said after the meeting is concluded. It is very likely that you will feel greatly relieved just to be better informed.

2.3 There is some information about my marriage that I think my attorney needs, but I'm too embarrassed to discuss it. Must I tell the attorney?

Your attorney has an ethical duty to maintain confidentiality. Past events in your marriage are matters that your lawyer is obligated to keep private. Attorneys who practice divorce law are accustomed to hearing a lot of intimate information about families. Although it is deeply personal to you, it is unlikely that anything you tell your lawyer will be a shock.

It may feel uncomfortable for a short moment, but it is important that your attorney have complete information so that your interests can be fully protected. If speaking directly about these facts still seems too hard, consider putting them in a letter.

2.4 I'm unsure about how to tell our children about the divorce, and I'm worried I'll say the wrong thing. What's the best way?

How you talk to your children about the divorce will depend upon their ages and development. Changes in your children's everyday lives, such as a change of residence or one parent leaving the home, are far more important to them.

Information about legal proceedings and meetings with lawyers are best kept among adults.

Simpler answers are best for young children. Avoid giving them more information than they need. Use the adults in your life as a source of support to meet your own emotional needs.

After the initial discussion, keep the door open to further talks by creating opportunities for them to talk about the divorce. Use these times to acknowledge their feelings and offer support. Always assure them that the divorce is not their fault and that they are still loved by both you and your spouse, regardless of the divorce.

2.5 My youngest child seems very depressed about the divorce, the middle one is angry, and my teenager is skipping school. How can I cope?

A child's reaction to divorce can vary depending upon his or her age and other factors. Some may cry and beg for a reconciliation, and others may behave inappropriately. Reducing conflict with your spouse, being a consistent and nurturing parent, and making sure both parents remain involved are all actions that can support your children regardless of how they are reacting to the divorce.

Support groups for children whose parents are divorcing are also available at many schools and religious communities. A school counselor can also provide support. If more help is needed, confer with a therapist experienced in working with children.

2.6 I am so frustrated by my spouse's "Disneyland parent" behavior. Is there anything I can do to stop this?

Feelings of guilt, competition, or remorse sometimes lead a parent to be tempted to spend parenting time in trips to the toy store and special activities. Other times these feelings can result in an absence of discipline in an effort to become the favored parent or to make the time "special."

Shift your focus from the other parent's behavior to your own, and do your best to be an outstanding parent during this time. This includes keeping a routine for your child for family meals, bedtimes, chores, and homework. Encourage family activities, as well as individual time with each child, when it's possible.

During the time when a child's life is changing, providing a consistent and stable routine in your home can ease his or her anxiety and provide comfort.

2.7   Between requests for information from my spouse's lawyer and my own lawyer, I am totally overwhelmed. How do I manage gathering all of this detailed information by the deadlines imposed?

First, simply get started. Often the thought about a task is worse than the job itself.

Second, break it down into smaller tasks. Perhaps one evening you gather your tax returns and on the weekend you work on your monthly living expenses.

Third, let in support. Ask that friend of yours who just loves numbers to come over for an evening with her calculator to help you get organized.

Finally, communicate with your lawyer. Your attorney or paralegal may be able to make your job easier by giving you suggestions or help. It may be that essential information can be provided now and the details submitted later.

2.8   I am so depressed about my divorce that I'm having difficulty getting out of bed in the morning to care for my children. What should I do?

See your health care provider. Feelings of depression are common during a divorce. You also want to make sure that you identify any physical health concerns.

Although feelings of sadness are common during a divorce, more serious depression means it's time to seek professional support.

Your health and your ability to care for your children are both essential. Follow through on recommendations by your health care professionals for therapy, medication, or other measures to improve your wellness.

2.9   Will taking prescribed medication to help treat my insomnia and depression hurt my case?

Not necessarily. Talk to your health care professional and follow their recommendations. Taking care of your health is of the utmost importance during this difficult time, and will serve your best interest as well as the best interest of your children. Inform your attorney of any medications that you are taking or treatment that you are seeking.

2.10 I know I need help to cope with the stress of the divorce, but I can't afford counseling. What can I do?

You are wise to recognize that divorce is a time for letting in support. You can explore a number of options, including:

- Meeting with a member of the clergy or lay chaplain
- Joining a divorce support group
- Turning to friends and family members
- Going to a therapist or divorce coach. If budget is a concern, contact a social agency that offers counseling services on a sliding-fee scale.

Additionally, there are several resources included at the back of this book that should be consulted to help determine if free counseling is available to you. Some health insurance plans provide coverage for counseling so ask the counselor if insurance might be an option. If none of these options are available, look again at your budget. You may see that counseling is important enough that you decide to find a way to increase your income or lower your expenses to support this investment in your well-being.

2.11 I'm the one who filed for divorce, but I still have loving feelings toward my spouse and feel sad about divorcing. Does this mean I should dismiss my divorce?

Strong feelings of caring about your spouse often persist after a divorce is filed. Whether or not to proceed with a divorce is a deeply personal decision. Although feelings can inform us of our thoughts, sometimes they can also cause us to not look at everything there is to see in our situation.

Have you and your spouse participated in marriage counseling? Has your spouse refused to seek treatment for an addiction? Are you worried about the safety of you or your children if you remain in the marriage? Can you envision yourself as financially secure if you remain in this marriage? Is your spouse involved in another relationship?

The answers to these questions can help you clarify whether to consider reconciliation. Talk to your therapist, coach, or spiritual advisor to help determine the right path for you.

2.12 Will my lawyer charge me for the time I spend talking about my feelings about my spouse and my divorce?

It depends. If you are paying your attorney by the hour, expect to be charged for the time your attorney spends talking with you.

2.13 My lawyer doesn't seem to realize how difficult my divorce is for me. How can I get him to understand?

Everyone wants support and compassion from the professionals who help during a divorce. Speak frankly with your attorney about your concerns. It may be that your lawyer does not see your concerns as being relevant to the job of getting your desired outcome in the divorce. Your willingness to improve the communication will help your lawyer understand how best to support you in the process and will help you understand which matters are best left for discussion with your therapist or a supportive friend.

2.14 I've been told not to speak ill of my spouse in front of my child, but I know she's doing this all the time. Why can't I just speak the truth?

It can be devastating for your child to hear you bad-mouthing his or her other parent. What your child needs is permission to love both of you, regardless of any bad parental behavior. The best way to support your child during this time is to encourage a positive relationship with the other parent.

2.15 Nobody in our family has ever been divorced and I feel really ashamed. Will my children feel the same way?

Making a change in how you see your family identity is huge for you. The best way to help your children is to establish a sense of pride in their new family and to look forward to the future with a real sense of possibility.

Your children will have an opportunity to witness you overcoming obstacles, demonstrating independence, and moving forward in your life despite the challenges. You can be a great teacher to them during this time by demonstrating pride in your family and in yourself.

2.16 I am terrified of having my deposition taken. My spouse's lawyer is very aggressive, and I'm afraid I'm going to say something that will hurt my case.

A deposition is an opportunity for your spouse's attorney to gather information and to assess the type of witness you will be if the case proceeds to trial. Feeling anxious about your deposition is normal. However, regardless of the personality of the lawyers, most depositions in divorces are uneventful.

Remember that your attorney will be seated by your side at all times to support you. Ask to meet with your lawyer in advance to prepare for the deposition. If you are worried about certain questions that might be asked, talk to your attorney about them. Think of it as an opportunity, and enlist your lawyer's support in being well prepared.

2.17 I am still so angry at my spouse; how can I be expected to sit in the same room during a settlement conference?

If you are angry with your spouse, it may be beneficial to postpone the conference for a time. You might also consider seeking some counseling to support you with coping with your feelings of anger.

Another option might be "shuttle" negotiations. With this method, you and your attorney remain in one room while your spouse and his or her attorney are in another. Settlement offers are then relayed between the attorneys throughout the negotiation process. By shifting your focus from your angry feelings to your goal of a settlement, it may be easier to proceed through the process.

2.18 I'm afraid I can't make it through court without having an emotional breakdown. How do I prepare?

A divorce trial can be a highly emotional time, calling for lots of support. Some of these ideas may help you through the process:

- Meet with your lawyer or the firm's support staff in advance of your court date to prepare you for court.

- Ask you lawyer whether there are any documents you should review in preparation for court, such as your deposition.
- Visit the courtroom in advance to get comfortable with the surroundings.
- Ask your lawyer about having a support person with you on your court date.
- Ask yourself what is the worst thing that could happen and consider what options you would have if it did.
- Avoid alcohol, eat healthfully, exercise, and have plenty of rest during the period of time leading up to the court date. Each of these will help you to prepare for the emotions of the day.
- Plan what you intend to wear in advance. Small preparations will lower your stress.
- Visualize the experience going well. Picture yourself sitting in the witness chair, giving clear, confident, and truthful answers to easy questions.
- Arrive early in the courthouse and make sure you have a plan for parking your car if you are not familiar with the area.
- Take slow, deep breaths. Breathing deeply will steady your voice, calm your nerves, and improve your focus.

Your attorney will be prepared to support you throughout the proceedings. By taking the above steps, you can increase the ease of your experience.

2.19   I am really confused. One day I think the divorce is a mistake; the next day I know I can't go back, and a few minutes later I can hardly wait to be single again. Some days I just don't believe I'm getting divorced. What's happening?

Denial, transition, and acceptance are common passages for a person going through a divorce. One moment you might feel excited about your future and a few hours later you think your life is ruined.

What can be helpful to remember is that you may not pass from one stage to the next in a direct line. Feelings of anger or sadness may well up in you long after you thought you had moved on. Similarly, your mood might feel bright one day as you think about your future plans, even though you may still miss your spouse.

Taking good care of yourself is essential during this period of your life. What you are going through requires a tremendous amount of energy. Allow yourself to experience your emotions, but also continue moving forward with your life. These steps will help your life get easier day by day.

3

Working with Your Attorney

If there is one thing you can be sure of in your divorce, it's that you will be given plenty of advice. Well-intentioned neighbors, cousins, and complete strangers will be happy to tell you war stories about their ex or about their sister who got divorced in Canada. Many will insist they know what you should do, even though they know nothing about the facts of your case or the current law in Kansas.

But there is one person whose advice will matter to you: your attorney. Your lawyer should be your trusted and supportive advocate at all times throughout your divorce. The counsel of your attorney can affect your life for years to come. You will never regret taking the time and energy to choose the right one for you.

See your relationship with your attorney as a partnership for pursuing what is most important to you. With clear and open attorney-client communication, you'll have the best outcome possible and your entire divorce will be less stressful.

By working closely with the right lawyer, you can trust the professional advice you receive and simply thank your cousin Millie for sharing.

3.1 Where do I begin looking for an attorney for my divorce?

There are many ways to find a divorce lawyer. Ask people you trust—friends and family members who have gone through a divorce, if they thought they had a good lawyer (or if their former spouse did!). If you know professionals who work with attorneys, ask for a referral to an attorney who is experienced in family law.

Consult your local bar association to find out whether they have a referral service. Be sure to specify that you are looking for an attorney who handles divorces.

Check with the law schools at Washburn University or the University of Kansas. A faculty member may be able to recommend a lawyer in your area.

Go online. Many attorneys have websites that provide information on their practices areas, professional associations, experience, and philosophy.

3.2   How do I choose the right attorney?

Choosing the right attorney for your divorce is an important decision. Your attorney should be a trusted professional with whom you feel comfortable sharing information openly. He or she should be a person you can trust and a zealous advocate for your interests.

You will rely upon your attorney to help you make many decisions throughout the course of your divorce. You will also entrust your legal counsel to make a range of strategic and procedural decisions on your behalf.

Consultation for a divorce might be your first meeting with a lawyer. Know that attorneys want to be supportive and to fully inform you. Feel free to seek all of the information you need to help you feel secure in knowing you have made the right choice.

Find an attorney who practices primarily in the family law area. Although many attorneys handle divorces, it is likely you will have more effective representation at a lower cost from an attorney who already knows the fundamentals of divorce law in Kansas.

Determine the level of experience you want in your attorney. For example, if you have had a short marriage, have young children, and few assets, an attorney with lesser experience might be a good value for your legal needs. However, if you are anticipating a custody dispute, have had a long-term marriage, or have complex or substantial assets, a more experienced attorney may better meet your needs.

Consider the qualities in an attorney that are important to you. Even the most experienced and skilled attorney is not right for every person. Ask yourself what you are really looking for in an attorney so you can make your choice with these standards in mind.

It is important that you be confident in the attorney you hire. If you're unsure about whether the lawyer is really listening to you or understanding your concerns, keep looking until you find one who will. Your divorce is an important matter. It's critical that you have a professional you can trust.

3.3   Should I hire a "bulldog"—a very aggressive attorney?

Again, consider the qualities in an attorney that are important to you. A "bulldog" may promise to be overly aggressive and take your spouse for everything he or she is worth. However, it may be important to you to create a mutually respectful relationship with your spouse during and after the divorce, especially if there are minor children involved.

Additionally, expect the cost of your divorce to exponentially increase if your attorney is unwilling to negotiate and drags your spouse into court at every opportunity. Look for a lawyer who can represent you with zealous advocacy, while maintaining a high level of courtesy, professionalism, and integrity.

3.4   Should I interview more than one attorney?

Be willing to interview more than one attorney. Every lawyer has different strengths, and it is important that you find the one that is right for you. Sometimes it is only by meeting with more than one attorney that you see clearly who will best be able to help you reach your goals in the way you want.

Changing lawyers in the middle of litigation can be stressful and costly. It is wise to invest energy at the outset in making the right choice.

3.5   My spouse says because we're still friends we should use the same attorney for the divorce. Is this a good idea?

Even the most amicable of divorcing couples usually have differing interests. For this reason, it is never recommended that an attorney represent both parties to a divorce. In most cases, an attorney is ethically prohibited from representing two people with conflicting interests who are in dispute.

Sometimes couples have reached agreements without understanding all of their rights under the law. A client often will benefit from receiving further legal advice on matters such as tax considerations, retirement, and health insurance issues.

It is not uncommon for one party to retain an attorney and for the other party not to do so. In such cases, the party with the attorney files the petition, and written agreements reached between the parties are typically sent to the spouse for approval prior to any court hearing. If your spouse has filed for divorce and said that you do not need an attorney, you should nevertheless meet with a lawyer for advice on how proceeding without a lawyer could affect your legal rights.

3.6 What information should I take with me to the first meeting with my attorney?

Attorneys differ on the amount of information they like to see at an initial consultation. If a court proceeding, either a divorce or a protection order, has already been initiated by either you or your spouse, it is important to take copies of any court documents.

If you have a prenuptial or postnuptial agreement with your spouse, that is another important document for you to bring at the outset of your case.

If you intend to ask for support, either for yourself or for your children, documents evidencing income of both you and your spouse will also be useful. These might include:

- Recent pay stubs
- Individual and business tax returns, W-2s, and 1099s
- Bank statements showing deposits
- A statement of your monthly budget

Your attorney will ask you to complete a questionnaire at or prior to the time of your first meeting. Preparing this questionnaire in advance can allow you to provide more complete information and to make the most of your appointment time with the lawyer.

If your situation is urgent or you do not have access to these documents, don't let it stop you from scheduling your appointment with an attorney. Prompt legal advice about your rights is often more important than having detailed financial information in the beginning. Your attorney can explain to you the options for obtaining these financial records if they are not readily available to you.

3.7 What unfamiliar words might an attorney use at the first meeting?

Law has a language all its own, and attorneys sometimes lapse into "legalese," forgetting that nonlawyers may not recognize words used daily in the practice of law. Some words and phrases you might hear include:

- *Dissolution of marriage*—the divorce
- *Petitioner*—person who files the divorce complaint
- *Respondent*—person who did not file the divorce complaint
- *Jurisdiction*—authority of a court to make rulings affecting a party
- *Service*—process of notifying a party about a legal filing
- *Discovery*—process during which each side provides information to each other
- *Decree*—the final order entered in a divorce

Never hesitate to ask your attorney the meaning of a term. Your complete understanding of your lawyer's advice is essential for you to partner with your advocate as effectively as possible.

3.8 What can I expect at an initial consultation with an attorney?

Most attorneys will ask that you complete a questionnaire prior to the meeting. With few exceptions, attorneys are required to keep confidential all information you provide.

The nature of the advice you get from an attorney in an initial consultation will depend upon whether you are still deciding whether you want a divorce, whether you are planning for a possible divorce in the future, or whether you are ready to file for divorce right away.

During the meeting, you will have an opportunity to provide the following information to the attorney:

- A brief history of the marriage
- Background information regarding yourself, your spouse, and your children
- Your immediate situation
- Your intentions and goals regarding your relationship with your spouse
- What information you are seeking from the attorney during the consultation

You can expect the attorney to identify the following information to you:

- The procedure for divorce in Kansas
- Identify the issues important in your case
- A preliminary assessment of your rights and responsibilities under the law
- Background information regarding the firm
- Information about fees and filings

Although some questions may be impossible for the attorney to answer at the initial consultation because additional information or research is needed, the initial consultation is an opportunity for you to ask all of the questions you have at the time of the meeting.

3.9 Will the communication with my attorney be confidential?

Yes. Your lawyer has an ethical duty to maintain your confidentiality. This duty of confidentiality also extends to the legal staff working with your attorney. The privileged information that you share with your attorney will remain private and confidential, unless such privilege is waived by voluntarily disclosing it to third parties.

3.10 Is there any way that I could waive the attorney-client privilege, as it relates to the duty of confidentiality?

Yes. To ensure that communications between you and your attorney remain confidential, and to protect against the voluntary or involuntary waiver of such privilege, below are some tips to consider:

- Refrain from disclosing the content of the communications with your attorney, or discussing in substantive detail the communications with your attorney with third parties. Such third parties can include friends and family members.

- Social media provides the potential for waiving the attorney-client privilege by publicly disclosing confidential information. Do not post information or send messages relating to your case on Facebook, Twitter, or other social media websites.

- Do not post information relating to your case or communications with your attorney on a personal blog, video blog, online chat rooms, or online message boards.

- Do not use your work-related e-mail to communicate with your attorney, or to discuss your case. Do not continue to use an e-mail account that your spouse has the password or access to the account.

- Depending upon your employer's policy relating to electronic communication, the attorney-client privilege may be waived by communicating with your attorney or by discussing your case through your personal e-mail account (G-mail, Yahoo, etc.) via a company computer. To ensure your communications remain confidential, it is best to communicate only via e-mail from your private e-mail address from your home computer.

3.11   Can I take a friend or family member to my initial consultation?

Yes. Having someone present during your initial consultation can be a source of great support. Recognize that having a support person in your consultation means that none of that consultation is attorney-client privileged and none of it is confidential. The support person could also become a witness in your case and could be requested to disclose your consultation to your spouse. If you are comfortable with that risk and lack of confidentiality, you might ask your support person to take notes on your behalf so that you can focus on listening and asking questions. Remember that this is your consultation, however, and it is important that the attorney hears the facts of your case directly from you. Be sure to ask your attorney how having a third party present at your consultation could impact the attorney-client privilege.

3.12 What exactly will my attorney do to help me get a divorce?

Your attorney will play a critical role in helping you get your divorce. You will be actively involved in some of the work, while other actions will be taken behind the scenes at the law office, the courthouse, or elsewhere.

Your attorney may perform any of the following tasks on your behalf:

- Assess the case to determine which court has jurisdiction to hear your divorce.
- Develop a strategy for advising you about all aspects of your divorce, including the treatment of assets and matters concerning children.
- Prepare legal documents for filing with the court.
- Conduct discovery to obtain information from the other party, which could include depositions, requests for production of documents, and written interrogatories.
- Appear with you at all court appearances, depositions, and conferences.
- Schedule all deadlines and court appearances.
- Support you in responding to information requests from your spouse.
- Inform you of actions you are required to take.
- Perform financial analyses of your case.
- Conduct legal research.
- Prepare you for court appearances and depositions.
- Prepare your case for hearings and trial, including preparing exhibits and interviewing witnesses.
- Advise you regarding your rights under the law.

- Counsel you regarding the risks and benefits of negotiated settlement as compared to proceeding to trial.

As your advocate, your attorney is entrusted to take all of
the steps necessary to represent your interests in the divorce.

3.13   What professionals should I expect to work with during my divorce?

Depending upon the issues identified by your attorney,
you can expect to work with various types of professionals,
such as appraisers, financial professionals, real estate agents,
and mental health experts.

Additionally, in some cases where custody or parenting
time issues are seriously disputed, the court may appoint a
guardian *ad litem* (GAL). This person, usually a lawyer, has the
duty to represent the best interest of the child. A guardian *ad
litem* has the responsibility to investigate you and your spouse
as well as the needs of your child. She or he may then present
recommendations or present witnesses and evidence to the
court of the best interest of the child.

As mentioned above, another expert who could be
appointed by the court is a psychologist. The role of the
psychologist will depend upon the purpose for which she
or he was appointed. For example, the psychologist may
be appointed to perform a child custody evaluation, which
involves assessing both parents and the child, or this expert
may be ordered to evaluate one parent to assess the child's
safety while spending time with that parent.

3.14   I've been divorced before and I don't think I need an attorney this time; however, my spouse is hiring one. Is it wise to go it alone?

Having gone through a prior divorce, it's likely that you
have learned a great deal about the divorce process as well as
your legal rights. However, there are many reasons why you
should be extremely cautious about proceeding without legal
representation.

It is important to remember that every divorce is different.
The length of the marriage, whether there are children, the
relative financial situation for you and your spouse, as well as
your age and health can all affect the financial outcome in your
divorce.

The law may have changed since your last divorce. Some aspects of divorce law are likely to change each year. New laws get passed and new decisions get handed down by the Kansas Supreme Court and the Kansas Court of Appeals that affect the rights and responsibilities of people who divorce.

In some cases, the involvement of your lawyer could be minimal. This might be the case if your marriage was short, your financial situation very similar to that of your spouse, there are no children, and the two of you remain amicable. At a minimum, have an initial consultation with an attorney to discuss your rights and have an attorney review any final agreement before you sign it.

3.15   Can I bring my children to meetings with my attorney?

It's best to make other arrangements for your children when you meet with your attorney. Your attorney will be giving you a great deal of important information during your conferences, and it will benefit you to give your full attention to the meeting.

It's also recommended that you take every measure to keep information about the legal aspects of your divorce away from your children. Knowledge that you are seeing an attorney can add to your child's anxiety about the process. It can also make your child a target for questioning by the other parent about your contacts with your attorney.

Most law offices are not designed to accommodate young children and are ordinarily not "childproof." For both your child's well-being and your own peace of mind, explore options for a trusted adult or family member to care for your child when you have meetings with your attorney.

3.16   What is the role of the *paralegal* or *legal assistant* in my attorney's office?

A *paralegal,* or *legal assistant,* is a trained legal professional whose duties include providing support for you and your lawyer. Working with a paralegal can make your divorce easier because he or she is likely to be very available to help you. It can also lower your legal costs, as the hourly rate for paralegal services is less than the rate for attorneys.

A paralegal is prohibited from giving legal advice. It is important that you respect the limits of the role of the paralegal if he or she is unable to answer your question because it calls for giving a legal opinion. However, a paralegal can answer many questions and provide a great deal of information to you throughout your divorce.

Paralegals can help you by receiving information from you, reviewing documents with you, providing you with updates on your case, and answering questions about the divorce process that do not call for legal advice.

3.17 My attorney is not returning my phone calls. What can I do?

You have a right to expect your phone calls to be returned by your lawyer. Here are some options to consider:

- Ask to speak to the paralegal or another attorney in the office.

- Send an e-mail or fax telling your lawyer that you have been trying to reach him or her by phone and explain the reason it is important that you receive a call.

- Ask the receptionist or legal assistant to schedule a phone conference for you to speak with your attorney at a specific date and time.

- Schedule a meeting with your attorney to discuss both the issue needing attention as well as your concerns about the communication.

Your attorney wants to provide good service to you. If your calls are not being returned, take action to get the communication with your lawyer back on track.

3.18 How do I know when it's time to change lawyers?

Changing lawyers is costly. You will incur legal fees for your new attorney to review information which is already familiar to your current attorney. You will spend time giving much of the same information to your new lawyer that you gave to the one you have discharged. A change in lawyers often results in delays in the divorce.

The following are questions to ask yourself when you're deciding whether to stay with your attorney or seek new counsel:

- Have I spoken directly to my attorney about my concerns?
- When I expressed concerns, did my lawyer take action accordingly?
- Is my lawyer open and receptive to what I have to say?
- Am I blaming my lawyer for bad behavior of my spouse or opposing counsel?
- Have I provided my lawyer the information needed for taking the next action?
- Does my lawyer have control over the complaints I have, or are they ruled by the law or the judge?
- Is my lawyer keeping promises for completing action on my case?
- Do I trust my lawyer?
- What would be the advantages of changing lawyers when compared to the cost?
- Do I believe my lawyer will support me to achieve the outcome I'm seeking in my divorce?

Every effort should be made to resolve concerns with your attorney. If you have made this effort and the situation remains unchanged, it may be time to switch lawyers.

3.19 Are there certain expectations that I should have when working with my legal team?

Yes, your legal team will be able to provide you with support and guidance during this process. There are certain actions you can expect your legal team to do for you during your divorce. A list of some of them follows.

Meet with you prior to the filing of a court action to advise you on actions you should take first. There may be important steps to take before you initiate the legal process. Your legal team can support you to be well prepared prior to initiating divorce.

Take action to obtain a temporary court order or to enforce existing orders. Temporary court orders are often needed to ensure clarity regarding rights and responsibilities while your divorce is pending. Your legal team can help you obtain a temporary order and ask the court to enforce its orders if there is a violation.

Explain the legal process during each step of your case. Understanding the legal process reduces the stress of your divorce. Your legal team can guide you each step of the way.

Listen to your concerns and answer any questions. Although only the attorneys can give you legal advice, everyone on your team is available to listen, to provide support, and to direct you to the right person who can help.

Support you in developing your parenting plan. Many parents do not know how to decide what type of parenting plan is best for their children. Your legal team can help you look at the needs of your children and offer advice based on their experience in working with families.

Support you in the completion of your discovery responses and preparing for depositions. The "discovery" process can be overwhelming for anyone. You will be asked to provide detailed information and many documents. Your legal team can make this job easier. Just ask. If your case involves depositions, your legal team will support you to be fully prepared for the experience.

Identify important issues, analyze the evidence, and advise you. Divorce is complex. Often there is a great deal of uncertainty. Your legal team can analyze the unique facts of your case and advise you based upon the law and their expertise.

Communicate with the opposing party's attorney to try to resolve issues without going to court, and to keep your case progressing. Although your attorney cannot control the actions of the opposing party or their lawyer, your attorney can always initiate communication as your advocate. Phoning, e-mailing, or writing to opposing counsel are actions your legal team can take to encourage cooperation and to keep your divorce moving forward at the pace you want without the expense of contested litigation. If your spouse is represented by an attorney, your attorney cannot contact your spouse directly.

Think creatively regarding challenges with your case and provide options for your consideration. At the outset, you may see many obstacles to reaching a final resolution. Your legal team can offer creative ideas for resolving challenges and help you to explore your options to achieve the best possible outcome.

Facilitate the settlement process. Although your legal team can never make the other party settle, your attorney can take action to promote settlement. They can prepare settlement proposals, invite settlement conferences, and negotiate zealously on your behalf.

3.20 Are there certain things my legal team will not be able to do?

Yes. Although there are many ways in which your legal team can support you during your divorce, there are also things your legal team will not be able to accomplish.

Force the other parent to exercise their parenting time. Your legal team cannot force a parent to exercise parenting time. However, be mindful that a chronic neglect of parenting time may be a basis for modifying your parenting plan. Tell your attorney if the other parent is repeatedly failing to exercise their parenting time.

Force the other party to respond to a settlement proposal. Your attorney may send proposals or make requests to opposing counsel; however, there is no duty to respond. After repeated follow-ups without a response, it may be clear no response is coming. At that time, your attorney will decide whether the issues merit court action. Both parties must agree on all terms for a case to be settled without a trial. If one party wants to proceed to trial, even over a single issue, he/she will be able to do so.

Control the tone of communication from opposing counsel or communications from the other party, or the other party's family members. Unfortunately, communication from the opposing attorney may sometimes appear rude, condescending, or demanding. Your legal team cannot stop an attorney from using these tactics.

Absent a pattern of harassment, your legal team cannot stop the other party or third parties from contacting you. If you do not want the contact, talk with your attorney about how to best handle the situation. Of course, appropriate communication regarding your children is always encouraged.

Ask the court to compensate you for every wrong done to you by the other party over the course of your marriage. Although your attorney will empathize that you do have valid complaints, please understand that focusing on the most important issues will yield the best outcome in the end. Raising numerous small issues may distract from your most important goals.

Remedy poor financial decisions made during the marriage. With few exceptions, the court's duty is to divide the marital estate as it currently exists. The judge will not attempt to remedy all past financial wrongs, such as overspending or poor investments by your spouse. If there is significant debt, consult with a debt counselor or bankruptcy lawyer.

Control how the other party parents your children during his/her parenting time. Each parent has strengths and weaknesses. Absent special needs of a child, most judges will not issue orders regarding bedtimes, amount of TV watching or playing video games, discipline methods, clothing, or diet. Of course, any suspected child abuse should be promptly discussed with your attorney.

Demand an accounting of how a parent uses court-ordered child support. Absent extraordinary circumstances, the court will not order the other parent to provide an accounting for the use of child support.

Leveraging money for rights regarding your children. Tactics oriented toward asserting custody rights as leverage toward attaining financial goals will be discouraged. Your legal team should negotiate parenting issues based solely on considerations related to your child, then, separately negotiate child support based on financial considerations.

Guarantee payment of child support and alimony. Enforcement of payment of support is only possible when it is court ordered. However, even with a court order, you may experience inconsistent timing of payment due to job loss or a refusal to pay. Talk with your attorney if a pattern of repeated missed payments has developed.

Collect child care and uninsured medical expenses if provisions of the decree are not complied with. If your decree requires you to provide documentation of payment of expenses to the other party and you fail to, you could be prohibited from collecting reimbursement for those expenses. Follow the court's orders regarding providing documentation to the other parent, even if they don't pay as they should.

Always keep records of these expenses and payments made by each parent, and keep copies of communications with the other parent regarding payment/reimbursement. It is much easier to keep these records on an ongoing basis than to get copies of old checks, day care bills, medical bills, and insurance documents at a later time.

4

Attorney Fees and Costs

Anytime you make a major investment, you want to know what the cost is going to be and what you are getting for your money. Investing in quality legal representation for your divorce is no different.

The cost of your divorce might be one of your greatest concerns. Because of this, you will want to be an intelligent consumer of legal services. You want quality, but you also want to get the best value for the fees you are paying.

Legal fees for a divorce can be costly and the total expense not always predictable. But there are many actions you can take to control and estimate the cost. Develop a plan early on for how you will finance your divorce. Speak openly with your lawyer about fees from the outset. Learn as much as you can about how you will be charged. Insist on a written fee or representation agreement that spells out the fee and cost arrangements.

By being informed, aware, and wise, your financial investment in your divorce will be money well spent to protect your future.

4.1 Can I get free legal advice from a lawyer over the phone?

Every law firm has its own policy regarding lawyers talking to people who are not yet clients of the firm. Most questions about your divorce are too complex for a lawyer to give a meaningful answer during a brief phone call.

Questions about your divorce require a complete look at the facts, circumstances, and background of your marriage. To obtain good legal advice, it's best to schedule an initial consultation with a lawyer who handles divorces. Most attorneys who focus their practice on family law do not provide free office consultations.

4.2 Will I be charged for an initial consultation with a lawyer?

It depends. Some young or inexperienced lawyers give free consultations, however most family law attorneys charge a fee. When scheduling your appointment, you should be told the amount of the fee. Payment is ordinarily due at the time of the consultation.

4.3 If I decide to hire an attorney, when do I have to pay him or her?

If your attorney charges for an initial consultation, be prepared to make payment at the time of your meeting. At the close of your consultation, the attorney may tell you the amount of the retainer or fee deposit needed by the law firm to handle your divorce. However, you are not expected to pay the retainer or fee deposit at the time of your first meeting unless you are ready to proceed. The retainer or fee deposit is paid after the lawyer has accepted your case, you have decided to hire the lawyer, and you are ready to proceed.

4.4 What exactly is a *retainer* or *fee deposit* and how much will mine be?

A *retainer* or *fee deposit* is a sum paid to your lawyer in advance for services to be performed and costs to be incurred in your divorce. This will be either an amount paid toward a "flat fee" for your divorce, or an advance credit for services that will be charged by the hour.

If your case is accepted by the law firm, expect the attorney to request a retainer or fee deposit following the initial consultation. The amount of the retainer may vary from hundreds of dollars to several thousand dollars, depending upon the nature of your case. Contested custody, divorces involving businesses, or interstate disputes, for example, are all likely to require higher retainers.

Other factors that can affect the amount of the retainer include the nature and number of the disputed issues.

4.5   Will my attorney accept my divorce case on a contingency fee basis?

No. A contingency fee is one that only becomes payable if your case is successful. In Kansas, all lawyers are prohibited from entering into a contingent fee contract in any divorce case. Your lawyer may not accept payment based upon securing your divorce, the amount of alimony or support awarded, or the division of the property settlement.

4.6   How much does it cost to get a divorce?

The cost of your divorce will depend upon many factors. Some attorneys perform divorces for a flat fee, but most charge by the hour. A flat fee is a fixed amount for the legal services being provided. A flat fee is more likely to be used when there are no children of the marriage and the parties have agreed upon the division of their property and debts. Most Kansas attorneys charge by the hour for divorces.

It is important that your discussion of the cost of your divorce begin at your first meeting with your attorney. It is customary for family law attorneys to request a retainer or fee deposit prior to beginning work on your case.

Be sure to ask your attorney what portion, if any, of the retainer is refundable if you do not continue with the case or if you terminate your relationship with the attorney.

4.7   What are typical hourly rates for a divorce lawyer?

In Kansas, most experienced attorneys who regularly practice in the divorce area charge from $200 per hour to more than twice that rate. The rate your attorney charges may depend upon factors such as skills, reputation, experience, exclusive focus on divorce and family law, and what other attorneys in the area are charging.

If you have a concern about the amount of an attorney's hourly rate, but you would like to hire the firm with which the attorney is associated, consider asking to work with an associate attorney in the firm who is likely to charge a lower rate. Associates are attorneys who ordinarily have less experience than the senior partners. However, they often are trained by the senior partners, are experienced, and are capable of handling your case.

4.8 If I can't afford to pay the full amount of the retainer, can I make monthly payments to my attorney?

Every law firm has its own policies regarding payment arrangements for divorce clients. Often these arrangements are tailored to the specific client. Most attorneys will require a substantial retainer to be paid at the outset of your case. Some attorneys may accept monthly payments in lieu of the retainer. Most will require monthly payments in addition to the initial retainer, or request additional retainers as your case progresses. Ask frank questions of your attorney to have clarity about your responsibility for payment of legal fees.

4.9 I agreed to pay my attorney a substantial retainer to begin my case. Will I still have to make monthly payments?

Ask your attorney what will be expected of you regarding payments on your account while the divorce is in progress. Get clear answers on whether monthly payments on your account are allowed or will be expected, whether it is likely that you will be asked to pay additional retainers, and whether the firm charges interest on past-due accounts. Regular payments to your attorney can help you avoid having a tremendously burdensome legal bill at the end of your case. Additionally, you may also be required to keep a minimum credit balance on your account to ensure your case is adequately funded for ongoing work by your legal team.

4.10 My lawyer gave me an estimate of the cost of my divorce and it sounds reasonable. Do I still need a written fee agreement?

Absolutely. Insist upon a written agreement with your attorney. This is essential not only to define the scope of the services for which you have hired your lawyer, but also to ensure that you have clarity about matters such as your attorney's hourly rate, whether you will be billed for certain costs such as copying, and when you can expect to receive statements on your account.

A clear fee agreement reduces the risk of misunderstandings between you and your lawyer. It supports you both in being clear about your promises to each other so that your focus can be on the legal services being provided rather than on disputes about your fees.

4.11 How will I know how the fees and charges are accumulating?

Be sure your written fee agreement with your attorney is completely clear about how you will be informed regarding the status of your account. If your attorney agrees to handle your divorce for a flat fee, your fee agreement should clearly set forth what is included in the fee.

Most attorneys charge by the hour for handling divorces. At the outset of your case, be sure your written fee agreement includes a provision for the attorney to provide you with regular statements of your account. It is reasonable to ask that these be provided monthly.

Review the statement of your account promptly after you receive it. Check to make sure there are no errors, such as duplicate billing entries. If your statement reflects work that you were unaware was performed, call for clarification. Your attorney's office should welcome any questions you have about services it provided.

Your statement might also include filing fees, court reporter fees for transcripts of court testimony or depositions, copy expenses, or interest charged on your account. If several weeks have passed and you have not received a statement on your account, call your attorney's office to request one. Legal fees can mount quickly, and it is important that you stay aware of the status of your legal expenses.

4.12 What other expenses are related to the divorce litigation besides lawyer fees?

Talk to your attorney about costs other than the attorney fees. Ask whether it is likely there will be filing fees, court reporter expenses, subpoenas, or expert-witness fees, mediation, or parenting class fees. Expert-witness fees can be a substantial expense, ranging from hundreds to several thousands of dollars, depending upon the type of expert and the extent to which he or she is involved in your case.

Speak frankly with your attorney about these costs so that together you can make the best decisions about how to use your budget for the litigation.

4.13 Who pays for the experts such as appraisers, accountants, psychologists, and mediators?

Costs for the services of experts, whether appointed by the court or hired by the parties, are ordinarily paid for by the parties.

In the case of the guardian *ad litem* who may be appointed to represent the best interest of your children, the amount of the fee will depend upon how much time this professional spends. The judge often orders this fee to be equally shared by the parties. However, depending upon the circumstances, one party can be ordered to pay the entire fee. If you can demonstrate *indigency,* that is, a very low income and no ability to pay, the other party may be ordered to pay your share of the guardian *ad litem* fee, subject to a later adjustment by the court at the conclusion of your case.

Psychologists either charge by the hour or set a flat fee for a certain type of evaluation. Again, the court can order one party to pay this fee or both parties to share the expense. It is not uncommon for a psychologist to request payment in advance and hold the release of an expert report until fees are paid.

Mediators either charge a flat fee per session or an hourly rate fee. Generally each party will pay one-half of the mediator's fee, which is paid prior to your mediation sessions.

The fees for many experts, including appraisers and accountants, will vary depending upon whether the individuals are called upon to provide only a specific service such as an appraisal, or whether they will need to prepare for giving testimony and appear as a witness at trial.

4.14 What factors will impact how much my divorce will cost?

Although it is difficult to predict how much your legal fees will be, the following are some of the factors that affect the cost:

- Whether there are children
- Whether child custody is agreed upon
- Whether there are novel legal questions
- Whether a pension plan will be divided between the parties
- The nature of the issues contested
- The number of issues agreed to by the parties
- The cooperation of the opposing party and opposing counsel
- The frequency of your communication with your legal team
- The ability of the parties to communicate with each other, as well as the client's ability to communicate with her attorney
- The promptness with which information is provided and/or exchanged between both the clients and the attorneys
- Whether there are litigation costs, such as fees for expert witnesses or court reporters
- The hourly rate of the attorney
- The time it will take to conclude your divorce

Communicating with your lawyer regularly about your legal fees will help you to have a better understanding of the overall cost as your case proceeds.

4.15 Will my attorney charge for phone calls and e-mails?

Unless your case is being handled on a flat-fee basis, you should expect to be billed for any communication with your attorney. Many of the professional services provided by lawyers are done by phone and by e-mail. This time can be spent giving legal advice, negotiation, or gathering information to protect your interests. These calls and e-mails are all legal services for which you should anticipate being charged by your attorney.

To make the most of your time during attorney phone calls, plan your call in advance. Organize the information you want to relay, your questions, and any concerns to be addressed. This will help you to be clear and focused during the phone call so that your fees are well spent. These same organizing techniques will also help you write clear and focused e-mails.

4.16 Will I be charged for talking to the staff at my lawyer's office?

It depends. Check the terms of your fee agreement with your lawyer. Whether you are charged fees for talking to nonlawyer members of the law office may depend upon their role in the office. For example, many law firms charge for the services of paralegals and law clerks.

Remember that nonlawyers cannot give legal advice, so it is important to respect their roles. Don't expect the receptionist to give you an opinion regarding whether you will win custody or receive alimony.

Your lawyer's support staff will be able to relay your messages and receive information from you. They may also be able to answer many of your questions. Allowing this type of support from within the firm is an important way to control your legal fees, too.

4.17 What is a *litigation budget,* and how do I know if I need one?

If your case is complex and you are anticipating substantial legal fees, ask your attorney to prepare a *litigation budget* for your review. This can help you to understand the nature of the services anticipated, the time that may be spent, and the overall amount it will cost to proceed to trial. The litigation budget will likely be comprised of a combination of your attorney and your legal team's hourly rates. It can also be helpful for budgeting and planning for additional retainers. Knowing the anticipated costs of litigation can help you to make meaningful decisions about which issues to litigate and which to consider resolving through settlement negotiations.

4.18   What is a *trial retainer* and will I have to pay one?

The purpose of the *trial retainer* is to fund the work needed to prepare for trial and for services the day or days of trial. A trial retainer is a sum of money paid on your account with your lawyer when it appears as though your case may not settle and is at risk for proceeding to trial.

Confirm with your attorney that any unearned portion of your trial retainer will be refunded if your case settles. Ask your lawyer whether and when a trial retainer might be required in your case so that you can avoid surprises and plan your budget accordingly.

4.19   How do I know whether I should spend the attorney fees my lawyer says it will require to take my case to trial?

Deciding whether to take a case to trial or to settle is often the most challenging point in the divorce process. This decision should be made with the support of your attorney.

When the issues in dispute are primarily financial, often the decision about settlement is related to the costs of going to trial. Get a clear understanding about just how far apart you and your spouse are on the financial matters and compare this to the estimated costs of going to trial. By comparing these amounts, you can decide whether a compromise on certain financial issues and certainty about the outcome would be better than paying legal fees and not knowing how your case will resolve.

4.20   Is there any way I can reduce some of the expenses of getting a divorce?

Litigation of any kind can be expensive, and divorces are no exception. The good news is that there are many ways that you can help control the expense. Here are some of them.

Put it in writing. If you need to relay information that is important but not urgent, consider providing it to your attorney by mail, or e-mail. This creates a prompt and accurate record for your file and takes less time than exchanging phone messages and talking on the phone.

Keep your attorney informed. Just as your attorney should keep you up to date on the status of your case, you need to do the same. Keep your lawyer advised about any major developments in your life such as plans to move, have someone move into your home, change your employment status, or buy or sell property.

During your divorce, if your contact information changes, be sure to notify your attorney. Your attorney may need to reach you with information, and reaching you in a timely manner may help avoid more costly fees later.

Obtain copies of documents. An important part of litigation includes reviewing documents such as tax returns, account statements, report cards, or medical records. Your attorney will ordinarily be able to request or subpoena these items, but many may be readily available to you directly upon request.

Consult your attorney's website. If your lawyer has a website, it may be a great source of useful information. The answers to commonly asked questions about the divorce process can often be found there.

Utilize support professionals. Get to know the support staff at your lawyer's office. Although only attorneys are able to give you legal advice, the receptionist, paralegal, legal secretary, or law clerk may be able to answer your questions regarding the status of your case. Just as your communication with your attorney, all communication with any professionals in a law firm is required to be kept strictly confidential.

Consider working with an associate attorney. Although the senior attorneys or partners in a law firm may have more experience, you may find that working with an associate attorney is a good option. Hourly rates for an associate attorney are typically lower than those charged by a senior partner. Frequently the associate attorney has trained under a senior partner and developed excellent skills as well as knowledge of the law. Many associate attorneys are also very experienced.

Discuss with the firm the benefits of working with a senior or an associate attorney in light of the nature of your case, the expertise of the respective attorneys, and the potential cost savings to you.

Leave a detailed message. If your attorney knows the information you are seeking, she or he can often get the answer before returning your call or e-mail. This not only gets your answer faster, but also reduces costs.

Discuss more than one matter during a call or e-mail. It is not unusual for clients to have many questions during litigation. If your question is not urgent, consider waiting to call or e-mail until you have more than one inquiry. Never hesitate to call or e-mail to ask any legal questions.

Provide timely responses to information requests. Whenever possible, provide information requested by your lawyer in a timely manner. This avoids the cost of follow-up action by your lawyer and the additional expense of extending the time in litigation.

Carefully review your monthly statements. Scrutinize your monthly billing statements closely. If you believe an error has been made, contact your lawyer's office right away to discuss your concerns.

Remain open to settlement. Be alert to recognize that when your disagreement concerns financial matters, the value of money in dispute may be less than the amount it will cost to go to trial. By doing your part, you can use your legal fees wisely and control the costs of your divorce.

4.21   I don't have any money and I need a divorce. What are my options?

If you have a low income and few assets, you may be eligible to obtain a divorce at no cost or minimal cost through one of the following organizations:

- Kansas Legal Services (commonly referred to as *Legal Aid*)
- Kansas University or Washburn School of Law Legal Clinic
- Kansas State Bar Association Lawyer Referral/Legal Services

These organizations have a screening process for potential clients, as well as limits on the nature of the cases they take. The demand for their services is also usually greater than the number of attorneys available to handle cases. Consequently, if you are eligible for legal services from one of these programs, you should anticipate being on a waiting list.

In short, if you have very little income and few assets, you are likely to experience some delay in obtaining a lawyer. If you believe you might be eligible for participation in one of these programs, inquire early to increase your opportunity to get the legal help you are seeking.

4.22   I don't have much money, but I need to get a divorce as quickly as possible. What should I do?

If you have some money and want to divorce as soon as possible, consider some of these options:

- Borrow the legal fees from friends or family. Often those close to you are concerned about your future and would be pleased to support you in your goal of having your rights protected. Although this may be uncomfortable to do, remember that most people will appreciate that you trusted them enough to ask for their help. If the retainer is too much money to request from a single individual, consider whether a handful of persons might each be able to contribute a lesser amount to help you reach your goal of hiring a lawyer.

- Charge the legal fees on a low-interest credit card or consider taking out a loan.

- Start saving. If your case is not urgent, consider developing a plan for saving the money you need to proceed with a divorce. Your attorney may be willing to receive and hold monthly payments until you have paid an amount sufficient to pay the initial retainer.

- Talk to your attorney about using money held in a joint account with your spouse.

- Find an attorney who will work with you on a monthly payment basis.

- Ask your attorney about your spouse paying for your legal fees.

Closely examine all sources of funds readily available to you, as you may have overlooked money that might be easily accessible to you. In Kansas, attorneys are not allowed to take your divorce case on a contingency fee basis.

Contact Kansas Lawyer Referral/Legal Services. Let them know you have some ability to pay and ask for help finding a lawyer who will take your case for a reduced fee.

Even if you do not have the financial resources to proceed with your divorce at this time, consult with an attorney to learn your rights and to develop an action plan for steps you can take between now and the time you are able to proceed.

Often there are measures you can take right away to protect yourself until you have the money to proceed with your divorce.

4.23 Is there anything I can do on my own to get support for my children if I don't have money for a lawyer for a divorce?

Yes. If you need support for your children, contact the District Court Trustee in your Kansas County for help in obtaining a child support order. Although they cannot help you with matters such as custody or property division, they can pursue support from your spouse for your children.

4.24 If my parent pays my legal fees, will my lawyer give my parent information about my divorce?

If someone else is paying your legal feels, discuss with your lawyer and the payor your expectations that your lawyer will honor the ethical duty of confidentiality. Without your permission, your attorney should not disclose information to others about your case.

However, if you authorize your attorney to speak with your family members, be aware that you will be charged for these communications. Regardless of the opinions of the person who pays your attorney fees, your lawyer's duty is to remain your zealous advocate. As the client, you are the decision maker for your case, not your family.

4.25 Can I ask the court to order my spouse to pay my attorney fees?

Yes. If you want to ask the court to order your spouse to pay any portion of your legal fees, be sure to discuss this with your attorney at the first opportunity. Most lawyers will treat the obligation for your legal fees as yours until the other party has made payment.

If your case is likely to require costly experts and your spouse has a much greater ability to pay these expenses than you, talk to your lawyer about the possibility of filing a motion with the court asking your spouse to pay toward these costs while the case is pending.

4.26 What happens if I don't pay my attorney the fees I promised to pay?

The ethical rules for lawyers allow your attorney to withdraw from representation if you do not comply with your fee agreement. Your attorney may also file an attorney's lien against any judgment awarded to you to pay any outstanding attorney's fees or costs to the firm. Consequently, it is important that you keep the promises you have made regarding your account.

If you are having difficulty paying your attorney's fees, talk with your attorney about payment options. Consider borrowing the funds, using your credit card, or asking for help from friends and family.

Above all, do not avoid communication with your attorney if you are having challenges making payment. Keeping in touch with your attorney is essential for you to have an advocate at all stages of your divorce.

5

The Discovery Process

Discovery is one of the least talked about steps in divorce, but it is often among the most important. *Discovery* is the pretrial phase in a lawsuit during which each party can obtain information and evidence from the opposing party. The purpose of discovery is to ensure that both you and your spouse have access to the same information. In this way, you can either negotiate a fair agreement or have all of the facts and documents to present to the judge at trial. The discovery process enables you and your spouse to meet on a more level playing field when it comes to settling your case or taking it to trial. You and your spouse both need the same information if you hope to reach agreement on any of the issues in your divorce. Similarly, a judge must know all of the facts to make a fair decision.

The discovery process may seem tedious at times because of the need to obtain and to provide lots of detailed information. Completing it, however, can give tremendous clarity about the issues in your divorce. Trust your lawyer's advice about the importance of having the necessary evidence as you complete the discovery process in order to reach your goals in your divorce.

5.1 What types of discovery might be done by my lawyer or my spouse's lawyer?

Types of discovery include:

- *Interrogatories*—which are written questions that must be answered under oath

58

- *Requests for production of documents*—asking that certain documents be provided by you or your spouse
- *Requests for admissions*—asking that certain facts be admitted or denied
- *Subpoena* of documents
- *Depositions*—in which questions are asked and answered under oath in the presence of a court reporter but outside the presence of a judge

Factors that can influence the type of discovery conducted in your divorce can include:

- The types of issues in dispute
- How much access you and your spouse have to needed information
- The level of cooperation in sharing information
- The budget available for performing discovery

Talk to your lawyer about the nature and extent of discovery anticipated in your case.

5.2   How long does the discovery process take?

Discovery can take anywhere from a few weeks to a number of months, depending upon factors such as the complexity of the case, the cooperation of you and your spouse, and whether expert witnesses are involved.

The *Kansas Rules of Discovery* provide that interrogatories, requests for production of documents, and requests for admissions be responded to within thirty days.

5.3   My lawyer insists that we conduct discovery, but I don't want to spend the time and money on it. Is it really necessary?

The discovery process can be critical to a successful outcome in your case for several reasons:

- It increases the likelihood that any agreements reached are based on accurate information.
- It provides necessary information for deciding whether to settle or proceed to trial.
- It supports the preparation of defenses by providing information regarding your spouse's care.

- It avoids surprises at trial, such as unexpected witness testimony.
- It ensures all potential issues are identified by your attorney.

Discuss with your attorney the intention behind the discovery being conducted in your case to ensure it is consistent with your goals and a meaningful investment of your legal fees.

5.4   I just received from my spouse's attorney interrogatories and requests that I produce documents. My lawyer wants me to respond within two weeks. I'll never make the deadline. What can I do?

Answering your discovery promptly will help move your case forward and help control your legal fees. There are steps you can take to make this task easier.

First, look at all of the questions. Many of them will not apply or your answers will be a simple "yes" or "no."

Ask a friend to help you. It is important that you develop the practice of letting others help you while you are going through your divorce. Chances are that you will make great progress in just a couple of hours with a friend helping you.

Break it down into smaller tasks. If you answer just a few questions a day, the job will not be so overwhelming.

Call your lawyer. Ask whether a paralegal in the office can help you organize the needed information or determine whether some of it can be provided at a later date.

Delay in the discovery process often leads to frustration by clients and lawyers. Do your best to provide the information in a timely manner with the help of others.

5.5   I don't have access to my documents and my spouse is being uncooperative in providing my lawyer with information. Can my lawyer request information directly from an employer or financial institution?

Yes, it may be possible to issue a subpoena directly to an employer or financial institution. A *subpoena* is a court order directing an individual or corporate representative to appear before the court or to produce documents in a pending lawsuit. In the discovery process, a subpoena is used to compel an individual or corporation to produce documents, papers, books, or other physical exhibits that constitute or contain evidence that is relevant to your case.

5.6 My spouse's lawyer intends to subpoena my medical records. Aren't these private?

Whether or not your medical records are relevant in your case will depend upon the issues in dispute. If you are requesting alimony or if your health is an issue in the dispute of child custody, these records may be relevant.

Talk with your lawyer about your rights. There are a number of options which may be available to prevent the disclosure of your information.

5.7 I own my business, will I have to disclose my business records?

Yes, you may be required to provide extensive records of your business in the discovery process. However, it is common for the court to protect the confidentiality of these records.

5.8 It's been two months since my lawyer sent interrogatories to my spouse, and we still don't have his answers. I answered mine on time. Is there anything that can be done to speed up the process?

The failure or refusal of a spouse to follow the rules of discovery can add to both the frustration and expense of the divorce process. Talk with your attorney about filing a *motion to compel,* seeking a court order that your spouse provides the requested information by a certain date. A request for attorney fees for the filing of the motion may also be appropriate.

Ask your lawyer whether a subpoena of information from an employer or a financial institution would be a more cost effective way to get needed facts and documents if your spouse remains uncooperative.

5.9 What is a *deposition?*

A *deposition* is the asking and answering of questions under oath, outside of court, in the presence of a court reporter. A deposition may be taken of you, your spouse, or potential witnesses in your divorce case, including experts. Both attorneys will be present. You and your spouse also have the right to be present during the taking of depositions of any witnesses in your case.

Depositions are not performed in every divorce. They are most common in cases involving contested custody, complex financial issues, and expert-witness testimony.

After your deposition is completed, the questions and answers will be transcribed, that is, typed by the court reporter exactly as given and bound into one or more volumes. You will be given an opportunity to read and make corrections to that transcript. Discuss this review and any corrections with your attorney.

5.10   What is the purpose of a deposition?

A deposition can serve a number of purposes such as:

- Supporting the settlement process by providing valuable information
- Helping your attorney determine who to use as witnesses at trial
- Aiding in the assessment of a witness's credibility, that is, whether the witness appears to be telling the truth
- Helping avoid surprises at the trial by learning the testimony of witnesses in advance
- Preserving testimony in the event the witness becomes unavailable for trial

Depositions can be essential tools in a divorce, especially when a case is likely to proceed to trial.

5.11   Will what I say in my deposition be used against me when we go to court?

Usually, a deposition is used to develop trial strategy and obtain information in preparation for trial. In some circumstances, a deposition may be used at trial. For this reason, it is important that you prepare for your deposition with the assistance of your attorney.

If you are called later to testify as a witness and you give testimony contrary to your deposition, your deposition can be used to *impeach* you by showing the inconsistency in your statements. It is important to review your deposition prior to your live testimony to ensure consistency and prepare yourself for the type of questions you may be asked.

5.12 Will the judge read the depositions?

Unless a witness becomes unavailable for trial or gives conflicting testimony at trial, it is unlikely that the judge will ever read the depositions.

5.13 How should I prepare for my deposition?

To prepare for your deposition, review the important documents in your case, such as the complaint, your answers to interrogatories, your financial affidavit, and any temporary hearing affidavits.

Gather all documents you've been asked to provide at your deposition. Deliver them to your attorney in advance of your deposition for copying and review. Talk to your attorney about the type of questions you can expect to be asked. Discuss with him or her any questions you are concerned about answering.

5.14 What will I be asked? Can I refuse to answer questions?

Questions in a deposition can cover a broad range of topics including your education, work, income, and family. The attorney is allowed to ask anything that is reasonably calculated to lead to the discovery of admissible evidence. If the question may lead to relevant information, it can be asked in a deposition, even though it may be inadmissible at trial. If you are unsure whether to answer a question, ask your lawyer and follow his or her advice.

Your attorney also may object to inappropriate questions. If there is an objection, say nothing until the attorneys discuss the objection. You will be directed whether or not to answer.

5.15 What if I give incorrect information in my deposition?

You will be under oath during your deposition, so it is very important that you be truthful. If you give incorrect information by mistake, contact your attorney as soon as you realize the error. If you lie during your deposition, you risk being impeached by the other lawyer during your divorce trial. This could cause you to lose credibility with the court, rendering your testimony less valuable.

5.16 What if I don't know or can't remember the answer to a question?

You may be asked questions about which you have no knowledge. It is always acceptable to say "I don't know" if you do not have the knowledge. Similarly, if you cannot remember, simply say so.

5.17 What else do I need to know about having my deposition taken?

The following suggestions will help you to give a successful deposition:

- Prepare for your deposition by reviewing and providing necessary documents and talking with your lawyer.
- Get a good night's sleep the night before. Eat a meal with protein to sustain your energy, as the length of depositions can vary.
- Arrive early for your deposition so that you have time to get comfortable with your surroundings.
- Relax. You are going to be asked questions about matters you know about. Your deposition is likely to begin with routine matters such as your educational and work history.
- Tell the truth, including whether you have met with an attorney or discussed preparation for the deposition.
- Stay calm. Your spouse's lawyer will be judging your credibility and demeanor. Do not argue with the attorneys.
- Listen carefully to the entire question. Do not try to anticipate questions or start thinking about your answer before the attorney has finished asking the question.
- Answer the question directly. If the question calls only for "yes" or "no," provide such an answer.

- Do not volunteer information. If the lawyer wants to elicit more information, he or she will do so in following questions.
- If you do not understand the question clearly, ask that it be repeated or rephrased. Do not try to answer what you *think* was asked.
- Take your time and carefully consider the question before answering. There is no need to hurry.
- If you do not know or cannot remember the answer, say so. That is an adequate answer.
- Do not guess. If your answer is an estimate or approximation, say so. Do not let an attorney pin you down to anything you are not sure about. For example, if you cannot remember the number of times an event occurred, say that. If the attorney asks you if it was more than ten times, answer only if you can. If you can provide a range (more than ten but less than twenty) with reasonable certainty, you may do so.
- If an attorney mischaracterizes something you said earlier, say so.
- Speak clearly and loudly enough for everyone to hear you.
- Answer all questions with words, rather than gestures or sounds. "Uh-huh" is difficult for the court reporter to distinguish from "unh-unh" and may result in inaccuracies in the transcript.
- If you need a break at any point in the deposition, you have the right to request one. You can talk to your attorney during such a break.
- Discuss with your lawyer in advance of your deposition whether you should review the transcript of your deposition for its accuracy or whether you should waive your right to review and sign the deposition.

Remember that the purpose of your deposition is to support a good outcome in your case. Completing it will help your case to move forward.

5.18 Are depositions always necessary? Does every witness have to be deposed?

Depositions are less likely to be needed if you and your spouse are reaching agreement on most of the facts in your case and you are moving toward a settlement. They are more likely to be needed in cases where child custody is disputed or where there are complex financial issues. Although depositions of all witnesses are usually unnecessary, it is common to take depositions of expert witnesses.

5.19 Will I get a copy of the depositions in my case?

Ask your attorney for copies of the depositions in your case. It will be important for you to carefully review your deposition if your case proceeds to trial.

6

Mediation and Negotiation

If your marriage was full of conflict, you might be asking how you can make the fighting stop. You picture your divorce as having vicious lawyers, an angry spouse, and screaming matches. You wonder if there is a way out of this nightmare.

Or, perhaps you and your spouse are parting ways amicably. Although you are in disagreement about how your divorce should be settled, you are clear that you want the process to be respectful and without hostility. You'd rather spend your hard earned money on your children's college education than legal fees.

In either case, going to trial and having a judge make all of the decisions in your divorce is not inevitable. In fact, most Kansas divorce cases settle without the need for a trial. Mediation and negotiation can help you and your spouse resolve your disputed issues and reach your own agreements without taking your case before the judge who will make your decisions for you.

Resolving your divorce through a mediated or negotiated settlement has many advantages. You can achieve a mutually satisfying agreement, a known outcome, little risk of appeal, and often enjoy significantly lower legal fees. Despite the circumstances which led to the end of your marriage, it might be possible for your divorce to conclude peacefully with the help of these tools.

6.1   What is the difference between *mediation* and *negotiation*?

Both mediation and negotiation are methods used to help you and your spouse settle your divorce by reaching agreement rather than going to trial and having the judge make decisions for you. These methods are sometimes referred to as *alternative dispute resolution* or *ADR*.

Mediation uses a trained mediator who is an independent, neutral third party. He or she is a skilled professional who can assist you and your spouse in the process. *Negotiation* involves lawyers for both you and your spouse. Lawyers for the spouses may also be present during mediation, although their involvement is usually less than in negotiation.

6.2   How are mediation and negotiation different from a collaborative divorce?

Collaborative law is a method of resolving a divorce case where both parties have a strong commitment to settling their disputes and avoiding litigation. You and your spouse each hire an attorney trained in the collaborative law process. You and your lawyers enter into an agreement which provides that in the event either you or your spouse decides to take the case to court both of you must terminate services with your collaborative lawyers and start anew.

Often spouses in the collaborative process enlist the support of other professionals, such as an independent financial advisor or coaches, to support them through the process. Although the process may be lengthy, it enables the focus to shift away from the conflict and toward finding solutions. The attorneys become a part of the team supporting settlement rather than advocates adding to the conflict.

Talk to your lawyer about whether your case would be well suited to the collaborative law process.

6.3   What is involved in the mediation process? What will I have to do and how long will it take?

The mediation process will be explained to you in detail by the mediator at the start of the mediation session. Mediation involves one or more meetings with you, your spouse, and the mediator. In some cases the attorneys will also be present.

Prior to meeting with you and your spouse in an initial mediation session, the mediator will conduct an individual initial screening session with each of you to assess your ability to communicate with each other and for domestic intimate partner abuse or other forms of intimidation or coercion. After the mediator's initial screening, he or she will decide whether you and your spouse should mediate together, or whether your mediation should take place separately.

The mediator will outline ground rules designed to ensure you will be treated respectfully and given an opportunity to be heard. In most cases, you and your spouse will each be given an opportunity to make some opening remarks about what is important to you in the outcome of your divorce.

How long the process of mediation continues depends upon many of the same factors that affect how long your divorce will take. These include how many issues you and your spouse disagree about, the complexity of these issues, and the willingness of each of you to work toward an agreement.

Your case could settle after just a couple of mediation sessions or it might require a series of meetings. It is common for the mediator to clarify at the close of each session whether the parties are willing to continue with another session.

6.4 My lawyer said that mediation and negotiation can reduce delays in completing my divorce. How can they do this?

When the issues in your divorce are decided by a judge instead of by you and your spouse, there are many opportunities for delay. These can include:

- Waiting for the trial date
- Having to return to court on a later, second date if your trial is not completed on the day it is scheduled
- Waiting for the judge's ruling on your case
- Needing additional court hearings after your trial to resolve disputes about the intention of your judge's rulings, issues that were overlooked, or disagreement regarding the language of the decree

Each one of these events holds the possibility of delaying your divorce by days, weeks, or even months. Mediating or negotiating the terms of your divorce decree can eliminate these delays.

6.5   How can mediation and negotiation lower the costs of my divorce?

If your case is not settled by agreement, you will be going to trial. If the issues in your case are complex, attorney's fees and other costs will increase considerably.

By settling your case without going to trial, you may be able to save thousands of dollars in legal fees. Ask your attorney for a litigation budget that sets forth the potential costs of going to trial, so that you have some idea of these costs when deciding whether to settle an issue or to take it to trial before the judge.

6.6   Are there other benefits to mediating or negotiating a settlement?

Yes. A divorce resolved by a mediated or negotiated agreement can have these additional benefits:

Recognizing common goals. Mediation and negotiation allow for brainstorming between the parties and lawyers. Looking at all possible solutions, even the impractical ones, invites creative solutions to common goals. For example, suppose you and your spouse both agree that you need to pay your spouse some amount of equity for the family home you will keep, but you have no cash to make the payment. Together, you might come up with a number of options for accomplishing your goal and select the best one. Contrast this with the judge who simply orders you to pay the money without considering all of the possible options.

Addressing the unique circumstances of your situation. Rather than using a one-size-fits-all approach as a judge might do, a settlement reached by agreement allows you and your spouse to consider the unique circumstances of your situation in formulating a good outcome. For example, suppose you disagree about the parenting times for the Thanksgiving holiday. The judge might order you to alternate the holiday each year, even though you both would have preferred to have your child share the day.

Creating a safe place for communication. Mediation and negotiation give each party an opportunity to be heard. Perhaps you and your spouse have not yet had an opportunity to share directly your concerns about settlement. For example, you might be worried about how the temporary parenting time arrangement is impacting your children, but have not yet talked to your spouse about it. A mediation session or settlement conference can be a safe place for you and your spouse to communicate your concerns about your children or your finances.

Fulfilling your children's needs. You may see that your children would be better served by you and your spouse deciding their future rather than by a judge who does not know, love, and understand your children like the two of you do.

Eliminating the risk and uncertainty of trial. If a judge decides the outcome of your divorce, you give up control over the terms of the settlement. The decisions are left in the hands of the judge. If you and your spouse reach agreement, however, you have the power to eliminate the risk of an uncertain outcome.

Reducing the risk of harm to your children. If your case goes to trial, it is likely that you and your spouse will give testimony that will be upsetting to each other. As the conflict increases, the relationship between you and your spouse inevitably deteriorates. This can be harmful to your children. Contrast this with mediation or settlement negotiations, in which you open your communication and seek to reach agreement. It is not unusual for the relationship between the parents to improve as the professionals create a safe environment for rebuilding communication and reaching agreements in the best interest of a child.

Having the support of professionals. Using trained professionals, such as mediators and lawyers, to support you can help you to reach a settlement that you might think is impossible. These professionals have skills to help you focus on what is most important to you, and shift your attention away from irrelevant facts. They understand the law and know the possible outcomes if your case goes to trial.

Lowering stress. The process of preparing for and going to court can be stressful. Your energy is also going toward caring for your children, looking at your finances, and coping with the emotions of divorce. You might decide that you would be better served by settling your case rather than proceeding to trial.

Achieving closure. When you are going through a divorce, the process can feel as though it is taking an eternity. By reaching agreement, you and your spouse are better able to put the divorce behind you and move forward with your lives.

6.7   Is mediation mandatory?

In many parts of Kansas, mediation may be required. Although mediation is not mandatory prior to filing for divorce in Kansas, mediation is often mandatory after a divorce filing if you have minor children and do not have an agreement on your parenting plan. Mediation is required to develop a plan for the children, such as custody and parenting time. However, talk to your attorney if you and your spouse have reached an agreement regarding your children, as it may be possible to waive any mediation requirement in your county.

6.8   My spouse abused me and I am afraid to participate in mediation. Should I participate anyway?

If you have been a victim of domestic violence by your spouse, it is important that you discuss the appropriateness of mediation with your attorney. Mediation may not be a safe way for you to reach agreement.

Prior to allowing mediation to proceed, any mediator should ask you whether you have been a victim of domestic violence. This is critical for the mediator to both assess your safety and to ensure that the balance of power in the mediation process is maintained.

Talk with your attorney if you have experienced domestic violence or if you feel threatened or intimidated by your spouse. If so, your case may be referred to an approved specialized mediator for parents involved in high conflict situations. It may be possible to mediate with you and your spouse in different rooms or during separate sessions.

If you feel threatened or intimidated by your spouse but still want to proceed with mediation, talk to your attorney about him or her attending the mediation sessions with you. Request to have the mediation occur at your lawyer's office, where you feel more comfortable. If you do participate in mediation, insist that your mediator have a good understanding of the dynamic of domestic abuse and how they can impact the mediation process.

6.9 What training and credentials do mediators have?

The background of mediators varies. Some are attorneys; many come from other backgrounds such as counseling. Ask your attorney for help in finding a qualified and experienced mediator who has completed training in mediating family law cases. The availability of mediators also varies depending upon where you live.

6.10 What types of issues can be mediated or negotiated?

Generally, all of the issues in your case can be mediated or negotiated. In some Kansas counties, mediation may be limited to custody or parenting plan issues only. However, in advance of any mediation or negotiation session, you should discuss with your lawyer which issues you want to be mediated or negotiated.

Many Kansas counties require that you participate in mediation of matters concerning your children unless you have an agreed parenting plan. Talk with your lawyer in advance of any mediation about custody to be absolutely clear about the impact of custody decisions on child support. Agreeing to certain custody terms can drastically reduce child support, and you should not negotiate on child custody and parenting time without having first fully discussed with your attorney its impact on child support.

You may decide that certain issues are nonnegotiable for you. Discuss this with your attorney in advance of any mediation or negotiation sessions so that he or she can support you in focusing the discussions on the issues you are open to looking at. Mediation and negotiation are typically more successful when both parties enter into the process with an open mind and willingness to consider different options and solutions.

Although mediation of issues other than custody and parenting time of your children are not required, talk with your lawyer if you would like to mediate other issues, such as a property distribution or financial support.

6.11 What is the role of my attorney in the mediation process?

The role of your attorney in the mediation process will vary depending upon your situation. Your attorney can assist you in identifying which issues will be discussed in mediation and which are better left to negotiation between the lawyers or to the judge.

If you have minor children, it is essential that you discuss with your attorney how equally sharing physical custody of your children can significantly lower child support. In all cases it is important that your attorney review any agreements discussed in mediation before a final agreement is reached.

6.12 How do I prepare for mediation?

Prior to attending a mediation session with your spouse, discuss with your attorney the issues you intend to mediate. In particular, be sure to discuss the impact of custody and parenting time arrangements on child support.

Enlist your attorney's support in identifying your intentions for the mediation. Make a list of the issues important to you. For example, when it comes to your child, you might consider whether it is your child's safety, the parenting time schedule, or the ability to attend your children's events which concerns you most.

Be forward looking. Giving thought to your desired outcomes while approaching mediation with an open mind and heart is the best way to move closer to settlement.

6.13 Do children attend the mediation sessions?

In nearly all cases your child will not participate in the mediation. However, your case might be an exception if you have an older child who is sufficiently mature to participate in the process. Both parents would have to agree to any additional participants in the mediation.

If you think your child should be at the mediation table, talk to your lawyer and your mediator about the potential risks and benefits of including him or her in the process.

6.14 I want my attorney to look over the agreements my spouse and I discussed in mediation before I give my final approval. Is this possible?

Yes. Before giving your written or final approval to any agreements reached in mediation, it is critical that your attorney review the agreements first. This is necessary to ensure that you understand the terms of the settlement and its implications. Your attorney will also review the agreement for compliance with Kansas law.

6.15 Who pays for mediation?

The cost of mediation must be paid for by you or your spouse. Often it is an equally shared expense. Expect your mediator to address the matter of fees before or at your first session.

6.16 What if mediation fails?

If mediation is not successful, you still may be able to settle your case through negotiations between the attorneys. Mediation can help narrow the issues remaining to be negotiated or to be submitted to the judge. You and your spouse can agree to preserve the settlements that were reached on certain issues and to take only the remaining disputed issues to the judge for trial.

6.17 What is a *settlement conference*?

A *settlement conference* can be a powerful tool for the resolution of your case. It is a meeting held with you, your spouse, and your lawyers with the intention of negotiating the terms of your divorce. In some cases, a professional with important information or expertise needed to support the settlement process, such as an accountant, also may participate.

Settlement conferences are most effective when both parties and their attorneys see the potential for a negotiated resolution and have the necessary information to accomplish that goal.

6.18 Why should I consider a settlement conference when the attorneys can negotiate through letters and phone calls?

A settlement conference can eliminate the delays which often occur when negotiation takes place through correspondence and calls between the attorneys. Rather than waiting days or weeks for a response, you can receive a response on a proposal in a matter of minutes.

A settlement conference also enables you and your spouse, if you choose, to use your own words to explain the reasoning behind your requests. You are also able to provide information immediately to expedite the process.

6.19 How do I prepare for my settlement conference?

Being well prepared for the settlement conference can help you make the most of this opportunity to resolve your case without the need to go to trial. Actions you should take include:

- Provide in advance of the conference all necessary information. If your attorney has asked you for a current pay stub, tax return, debt amounts, asset values, or other documentation, make sure it is provided prior to the meeting.

- Discuss your topics of concern with your attorney in advance. Your lawyer can assist you in understanding your rights under the law so that you can have realistic expectations for the outcome of negotiations.

- Bring a positive attitude, a listening ear, and an open mind. Come with the attitude that your case will settle. Be willing to first listen to the opposing party, and then to share your position. To encourage your spouse to listen to your position, listen to hers or his first. Resist the urge to interrupt.

Few cases settle without each side demonstrating flexibility and a willingness to compromise. Most cases settle when the parties are able to bring these qualities to the process. A winner-takes-all approach is rarely successful.

6.20   What will happen at my settlement conference?

Typically the conference will be held at the office of one of the attorneys, with both parties and lawyers present. If there are a number of issues to be discussed, an agenda may be used to keep the focus on relevant topics. From time to time throughout the conference, you and your attorney may meet alone to consult as needed. If additional information is needed to reach agreement, some issues may be set aside for later discussion.

The length of the conference depends upon the number of issues to be resolved, the complexity of the issues, and the willingness of the parties and lawyers to communicate effectively. An effort is made to confirm which issues are resolved and which issues remain disputed. Then, one by one the issues are addressed.

6.21   What is the role of my attorney in the settlement conference?

Your attorney is your advocate during the settlement conference. You can count on him or her to support you throughout the process, to see that important issues are addressed, and to counsel you privately outside of the presence of your spouse and his or her lawyer.

6.22   Why is my lawyer appearing so friendly with my spouse and the other lawyer?

Successful negotiations rely upon building trust between the parties working toward agreement. Your lawyer may be respectful or pleasant toward your spouse or your spouse's lawyer to promote a good outcome for you.

6.23   What happens if my spouse and I settled some but not all of the issues in our divorce?

You and your spouse can agree to maintain the agreements you have reached and let the judge decide just those matters which you are unable to resolve.

6.24   If my spouse and I reach an agreement, how long will it take before it can be finalized?

If a settlement is reached through negotiation or mediation, one of the attorneys will put the agreement in writing for approval by you and your spouse. The drafting process can take several days to several weeks to complete. If you or your spouse request a final hearing and the sixty-day waiting period has expired, in most cases, a final hearing is held within thirty days of the agreement being signed. If there is not a final hearing, your agreement is submitted to the judge for approval and is usually finalized in several business days.

What to bring to Oct 3 mtg to save time

How long = mediation is divorce finalized

can we have say in when I must move

When do assets get divided; how is it worth

7

Emergency:
When You Fear Your Spouse

Suddenly you are in a panic. Maybe your spouse was serious when threatening to take your child and leave the state. What if you're kicked out of your own home?

Suppose all of the bank accounts are emptied? Your fear heightens as your mind spins with every horror story you've ever heard about divorce.

Facing an emergency situation in divorce can feel as though your entire life is at stake. You may not be able to concentrate on anything else. At the same time, you may be paralyzed with anxiety and have no idea how to begin to protect yourself. No doubt you have countless worries about what your future holds.

Remember that you have overcome many challenges in your life before this moment. There are people willing to help you. You have strength and wisdom you may not yet even realize. Step by step, you will make it through this time.

When facing an emergency, do your best to focus on what to do in the immediate moment. Set aside your worries about the future for another day. Now it is time to stay in the present moment, let others support you, and start taking action right away.

7.1 My spouse has deserted me, and I need to get divorced as quickly as possible. What is my first step?

Your first step is to seek legal advice at your earliest opportunity. The earlier you get legal counsel to advise you about your rights, the better. The initial consultation will answer most of your questions and start you on an action plan for getting your divorce underway.

7.2 I'm afraid my abusive spouse will try to hurt me and/ or our children if I say I want a divorce. What can I do legally to protect myself and my children?

Develop a plan with your safety and that of your children as your highest priority. In addition to meeting with an attorney at your first opportunity, develop a safety plan in the event you and your children need to escape your home. A great way to do this is to seek support from an agency that helps victims of domestic violence. Call the National Domestic Violence Hotline at (800) 799-7233 to get more information about the domestic violence program closest to you.

Your risk of harm from an abusive spouse increases when you leave. For this reason, all actions must be taken with safety as the first concern.

Find a lawyer who understands domestic violence. Often your local domestic violence agency can help with a referral. Talk to your lawyer about the concerns for your safety and that of your children. Ask your lawyer about a *protection order*. This is a court order which may offer a number of protections including granting you temporary custody of your children and ordering your spouse to leave the family residence and have no contact with you.

7.3 I am afraid to meet with a lawyer because I am terrified my spouse will find out and get violent. What should I do?

Schedule an initial consultation with an attorney who is experienced in working with domestic violence victims. When you schedule the appointment, let the firm know your situation and instruct the law office not to place any calls to you which you think your spouse might discover. If possible, pay for your consultation in cash.

Consultations with your attorney are confidential. Your lawyer has an ethical duty to not disclose your meeting with anyone outside of the law firm. Let your attorney know your concerns so that extra precautions can be taken by the law office in handling your file.

7.4   I want to give my attorney all the information needed so my children and I are safe from my spouse. What does this include?

Provide your attorney with complete information about the history, background, and nature and evidence of your abuse including:

- The types of abuse (for example, physical, sexual, verbal, financial, mental, emotional)
- The dates, time frames, or occasions
- The locations
- Whether you were ever treated medically
- Any police reports made
- E-mails, letters, notes, or journal entries
- Any photographs taken
- Any witnesses to the abuse or evidence of the abuse
- Any statements made by your spouse admitting the abuse
- Alcohol or drug abuse
- The presence of guns or other weapons

The better the information you provide to your lawyer, the easier it will be for him or her to make a strong case for the protection of you and your children.

7.5   I'm not ready to hire a lawyer for a divorce, but I am afraid my spouse is going to get violent with my children and me in the meantime. What can I do?

It is possible to seek a protection order from the court without an attorney. It is possible for the judge to order your spouse out of your home, granting you custody of your children, and to order your spouse to stay away from you.

7.6   What are the differences between a *domestic abuse protection order*, a *stalking protection order*, and a *restraining order*?

Protection orders and r*estraining orders* are court orders directing a person to not engage in certain behavior. Each of them can be used to protect the person who obtained the order from the threats or actions of others. Although any of the orders

81

can initially be obtained without notice to the other person, there is always a right to a hearing to determine whether a protection order or restraining order should remain in place.

Talk to your attorney about obtaining a *domestic abuse protection order* if you are concerned about your safety, your children's safety, or if there has been a history of domestic abuse. If your spouse has attempted to cause, has caused you bodily injury, or has threatened to cause you bodily injury, you may qualify for a domestic abuse protection order. The violation of a domestic abuse protection order is a criminal offense, which can result in immediate arrest.

If your spouse has engaged in conduct that seriously terrifies, threatens, or intimidates you, speak with your attorney about the possibility of obtaining a *harassment* or *stalking protection order.* Some examples of harassment that qualify for protection under a stalking protection order include following, stalking, harassment, or repeatedly contacting you. The violation of a stalking protection order is also a criminal offense, which can result in an immediate arrest.

If you are concerned that your spouse will annoy, threaten, harass, or intimidate you after your divorce complaint is filed, or during the divorce case, ask your lawyer about a *restraining order.* A restraining order is a court order that prohibits a person from engaging in behavior that has been restrained by the court. If your spouse violates the restraining order, he or she may be brought before the court for contempt.

7.7 My spouse has never been violent, but I know she is going to be really angry and upset when the divorce papers are served. Do I need a protection order?

The facts of your case may not warrant a protection order. However, if you are still concerned about your spouse's behavior, ask your attorney about a *temporary restraining order (TRO)* to be delivered to your spouse at the same time as the divorce complaint. This court order directs your spouse not to annoy, threaten, intimidate, or harass you while the divorce is in progress. A temporary restraining order can also order your spouse not to sell or transfer assets until your divorce is completed.

7.8   My spouse has been harassing me since I filed for divorce. What can I do?

It may be possible to seek a protection order from the court. In order to qualify for a protection order, you must be able to prove that your spouse has engaged in a knowing and willful course of conduct that seriously terrifies, threatens, or intimidates you. Talk with your lawyer about whether you should seek the court's protection from your spouse.

7.9   I'm afraid my spouse is going to take all of the money out of the bank accounts and leave me with nothing. What can I do?

Talk to your attorney immediately. If you are worried about your spouse emptying financial accounts or selling marital assets, it is critical that you take action at once. Your attorney can advise you on your right to take possession of certain assets in order to protect them from being hidden or spent by your spouse.

Ask your lawyer about seeking a temporary restraining order (TRO). This order forbids your spouse from selling, transferring, hiding, or otherwise disposing of marital property until the divorce is complete.

A temporary restraining order is intended to prevent assets from "disappearing" before a final division of the property from your marriage is complete. If this is a concern, talk to your lawyer about the benefits of obtaining a temporary restraining order as to property prior to giving your spouse notice that you are filing for divorce.

7.10   My spouse says that I am crazy, that I am a liar, and that no judge will ever believe me if I tell the truth about the abusive behavior. What can I do if I don't have any proof?

Most domestic violence is not witnessed by third parties. Often there is little physical evidence. Even without physical evidence, a judge can enter orders to protect you and your children if you give truthful testimony about your abuse which the judge finds believable. Your own testimony of your abuse is evidence.

It is very common for persons who abuse others to claim that their victims are liars and to make statements intended to discourage disclosure of the abuse. This is yet another form of controlling behavior.

Your attorney's skills and experience will support you to give effective testimony in the courtroom to establish your case. Let your lawyer know your concerns so that a strong case can be presented to the judge based upon your persuasive statements of the truth of your experience.

7.11 My spouse told me that if I ever file for divorce, I'll never see my child again. Should I be worried about my child being abducted?

Your fear that your spouse will abduct your child is a common one. It can be helpful to look at some of the factors that appear to increase the risk that your child will be removed from the state by the other parent.

Most abductions are made by men. They are often from marriages that cross culture, race, religion, or ethnicity. A lower socioeconomic status, prior criminal record, and limited social or economic ties to the community can also increase risk.

Programming and brainwashing are almost always present in cases where a child is at risk for being kidnapped by a parent, and efforts to isolate the child may also be seen. Exit activities such as obtaining a new passport, getting financial matters in order, or contacting a moving company could be indicators.

Talk to your lawyer to assess the risks in your particular case. Together you can determine whether statements by your spouse are threats intended to control or intimidate you or whether legal action is needed to protect your child.

7.12 What legal steps can be taken to prevent my spouse from removing our child from the state?

If you are concerned about your child being removed from the state, ask your lawyer whether any of these options might be available in your case:

- A court order giving you immediate custody until a temporary custody hearing can be held

- A court order directing your spouse to turn over passports for the child and your spouse to the court
- The posting of a bond prior to your spouse exercising parenting time
- Supervised visitation

Both state and federal laws are designed to provide protection from the removal of children from one state to another when a custody matter is brought and to protect children from kidnapping. The *Uniform Child Custody Jurisdiction Enforcement Act (UCCJEA)* was passed to encourage the custody of children to be decided in the state where they have been living most recently and where they have the most ties. The *Parental Kidnapping Prevention Act (PKPA)* makes it a federal crime for a parent to kidnap a child in violation of a valid custody order.

If you are concerned about your child being abducted, talk with your lawyer about all options available to you for your child's protection.

7.13 How quickly can I get a divorce in Kansas?

There are a number of time requirements for getting a divorce in Kansas. Either you or your spouse must have been a resident of Kansas for more than sixty days immediately prior to the filing of the complaint for the divorce with the court. After you file your divorce, your spouse must be given notice of the divorce.

A sixty-day waiting period is required for every Kansas divorce. This period begins on the date the divorce complaint is filed with the court.

The soonest your case can be resolved is after the sixty-day waiting period has expired, although most cases do not resolve this quickly. The length of time your case remains pending depends in large part upon the extent to which you and your spouse reach agreement on the issues in your case.

Your divorce becomes final for most purposes thirty days after the judge signs your divorce decree. With electronic filing in most courts, the judge's signature may be electronic. However, you may not remarry for a period of thirty days after your decree is entered with the clerk of the court.

7.14   I really need a divorce quickly. Will the divorce I get in another country be valid in Kansas?

If both you and your spouse regard Kansas as your true home and you both intend to remain in the state, a divorce from another state or country may not be valid. If Kansas is the permanent home for both of you, you generally cannot obtain a divorce in another state or country, even if you reside there temporarily.

7.15   If either my spouse or I file for divorce, will I be ordered out of my home? Who decides who gets to live in the house while we go through the divorce?

If you and your spouse cannot reach an agreement regarding which of you will leave the residence during the divorce, the judge will decide whether one of you should be granted exclusive possession of the home until the case is concluded. In some cases judges have been known to refuse to order either party out of the house until the divorce is concluded.

Abusive behavior is one basis for seeking temporary possession of the home. If there are minor children, the custodial parent will ordinarily be awarded temporary possession of the residence.

Other factors the judge may consider include:

- Whether one of you owned the home prior to the marriage
- After provisions are made for payment of temporary support, who can afford to remain in the home or obtain other housing
- Who is most likely to be awarded the home in the divorce
- Options available to each of you for other temporary housing, including other homes or family members who live in the area
- Special needs that would make a move unduly burdensome, such as a health condition
- Self-employment from home, which could not be readily moved, such as a child-care business

If staying in the home is important to you, talk to your attorney about your reasons so that a strong case can be made for you at the temporary hearing.

8

Child Custody

Ever since you and your spouse began talking about divorce, chances are your children have been your greatest concern. You or your spouse might have postponed the decision to seek divorce because of concern about the impact on your children. Now that the time has come, to separate or divorce, you might still have doubts about whether your children will be all right after the divorce.

Remember that you have been making wise and loving decisions for your children since they were born. You've always done your best to see that they had everything they really needed. You loved them and protected them. This won't change because you are going through your divorce. You were a good parent before the divorce and you will be a good parent after the divorce.

It can be difficult not to worry about how the sharing of parenting time with your spouse will affect your children. You may also have fears about being cut out of your child's life. Try to remember that it is likely that the court order will not only give you a lot of time with your children but also a generous opportunity to be involved in their day-to-day lives.

With the help of your lawyer, you can make sound decisions regarding the custody arrangement that is in the best interest of your children.

8.1   What types of custody are awarded in Kansas?

Under Kansas law, there are two aspects to a custody determination. These are *legal custody* and *physical custody*.

Legal custody refers to the rights and responsibilities to make fundamental decisions regarding your children, such as which school they attend, what religion or church they are involved in, and who their health care providers are.

Legal custody may be awarded to you, to your spouse, or in all but the most rare circumstances to both of you jointly. In the extraordinary situation, if you have sole legal custody, you are the primary and final decision maker for the fundamental decisions regarding your children. *Joint legal custody* means that you and your former spouse will share equally in the fundamental decision making for your child. If you and the other parent are unable to reach agreement, you may need to return to mediation or to court for the decision to be made.

Joint legal custody is presumed to be in the best interest of your child in Kansas. It generally requires:

- Effective and open communication between the parents concerning the child
- Both parents to continue to co-parent together
- A willingness on the part of both parents to place the child's needs before their own
- Both parents' willingness to be flexible and compromising about making decisions concerning the child

Physical custody refers to the physical location of the children, that is, where they spend their time. In Kansas physical custody is called *parenting time*. Like legal custody, parenting time may be awarded to either parent or to both parents jointly. Equal parenting time is referred to as "shared parenting time" physical custody. Notwithstanding who has legal custody, the parent who is with the children will make the day-to-day decisions regarding their care during their parenting time.

Specific parenting time will always be awarded to each parent. Provisions for days of the week, school breaks, summer, holidays, and vacations are typically made in detail. In the event that one of your children will reside with you and another child will reside with the other parent, the arrangement is referred to as *split* or *divided parenting time*.

Be sure to discuss with your attorney not only the best interest of your child, but also the possible ramifications of custody to child support. An award of shared parenting time (50/50 time) can result in a substantial reduction in any child support.

8.2   On what basis will the judge award custody?

The judge considers many factors in determining child custody. Most important is "the best interest of the child." To determine best interest, the judge may look at the following factors:

Home environments. This refers to the respective environments offered by you and your spouse. The court may consider factors such as the safety, stability, and nurturing found in each home.

Emotional ties. The emotional relationship between the child and each parent may include the nature of the bond between the parent and child and the feelings shared between the child and each parent.

Age, sex, and health of the child and parents. Kansas no longer ascribes to the "tender years" doctrine, which formerly gave a preference for custody of very young children to the mother. If one of the parents has an illness that may impair the ability to parent, it may be considered by the court. Similarly, the judge may look at special health needs of a child.

Effect on the child of continuing or disrupting an existing relationship. This factor might be applied in your case if you stayed at home for a period of years to care for your child, and awarding custody to the other parent would disrupt your relationship with your child.

Attitude and stability of each parent's character. The court may consider your ability and willingness to be cooperative with the other parent in deciding who should be awarded custody. The court may also consider each parent's history, which reflects the stability of his or her character.

Moral fitness of each parent, including sexual conduct. The extent to which a judge assesses the morals of a parent can vary greatly from judge to judge. Sexual conduct will ordinarily not be considered unless it has harmed your child or your child was exposed to sexual conduct.

Capacity to provide physical care and satisfy educational needs. Here the court may examine whether you or the other parent is better able to provide for your child's daily needs such as nutrition, health care, hygiene, social activities, and education. The court may also look to see whether you or your spouse has been attending to these needs in the past.

Preferences of the child. The child's preference regarding custody may be considered if the child is of sufficient age of comprehension, regardless of chronological age, and the child's preference is based on sound reasoning. Kansas, unlike some other states, does not allow a child to choose the parent he or she wishes to live with. Rather, the court may consider the well-reasoned preferences of a child, at any age. Typically, the older the child, the greater the weight given to the preference. However, the child's reasoning is also important. For further explanation, please see question 8.5

Health, welfare, and social behavior of the child. Every child is unique. Your child's needs must be considered when it comes to deciding custody and parenting time. The custody of a child with special needs, for example, may be awarded to the parent who is better able to meet those needs.

The judge may also consider whether you or your spouse has fulfilled the role of primary care provider for meeting the day-to-day needs of your child.

Domestic violence. Domestic violence is an important factor in determining custody, as well as parenting time and protection from abuse during the transfer of your child to the other parent. If domestic violence is a concern in your case, be sure to discuss it in detail with your attorney during the initial consultation so that every measure can be taken to protect the safety of you and your children.

8.3   What's the difference between *visitation* and *parenting time?*

Historically, time spent with the noncustodial parent was referred to as *visitation.* Today, the term *parenting time* is used to refer to the time a child spends with either parent.

This change in language reflects the intention that children spend time with both parents and have two homes, as opposed to their living with one parent and visiting the other.

8.4 How can I make sure I will get to keep the children during the divorce proceedings?

You cannot ensure that your children will stay with you during the divorce process. However, the best way to provide clarity about the living arrangements and respective parenting time with your children during your divorce is to obtain a temporary order. Informal agreements between parties cannot always be trusted. Additionally, informal agreements with your spouse lack the ability to be enforced by the court. Thus, even if you and your spouse have agreed to temporary arrangements, talk with your attorney about whether this agreement should be formalized in a court order.

Obtaining a temporary order can be an important protection not only for the custody of your children, but also for other issues such as financial support, temporary exclusive possession of the marital home, temporary protection from your spouse, or attorney's fees.

Until a temporary order is entered, it's best that you continue to reside with your children. If you are considering leaving your home, talk with your attorney before making any significant changes to your living situation. If you must leave your home, take your children with you and talk with your attorney at your earliest opportunity.

8.5 How much weight does the child's preference carry?

The preference of your child is only one of many factors a judge may consider in determining custody. The age of your child and his or her ability to express the underlying reason for their preference to live with either parent will determine the amount of weight the judge will give to your child's preference. Although there is no age at which your child's preference determines custody, most judges will give more weight to the wishes of an older child. Most judges will not interview a younger child.

The reasoning underlying your child's preference is also a factor to consider. Consider the fifteen-year-old who wants to live with mother because "Mom lets me stay out past curfew, I get a bigger allowance, and I don't have to do chores." Greater weight might be given to the preference of an older teenager who wants to live with mother because "she helps me with my homework, attends all of my band performances, and doesn't call me names like Dad does."

If you see that your child's preference may be a factor in the determination of custody, discuss it with your lawyer so that this consideration is a part of assessing the action to be taken in your case.

8.6 How old do the children have to be before they can speak to the judge about with whom they want to live?

It depends upon the judge. There is no set age at which children are allowed to speak to the judge about their preferences as to custody. Most judges will not interview a child who is not a teenager.

If either you or your spouse wants the judge to listen to what your child has to say, a request is ordinarily made to the judge to have the child speak to the judge in the judge's office (chambers) rather than from the witness stand. Depending upon the judge's decision, the attorneys for you and your spouse may also be present.

It is possible that the judge may also allow the attorneys to question the child. If you have concerns about the other parent learning what your child says to the judge, talk to your lawyer about the possibility of obtaining a directive from the court to keep this information confidential.

Typically the testimony of the child is made "on the record," that is, in the presence of a court reporter. This is so the testimony can be transcribed later in the event of an appeal.

In addition to the age of a child, a judge may consider such facts as the child's maturity and personality in determining whether an interview of the child by the judge will be helpful to the custody decision-making process.

8.7 How can I prove that I was the primary care provider?

One tool to assist you and your attorney in establishing your case as a primary care provider is a chart indicating the care you and your spouse have each provided for your child. The clearer you are about the history of parenting, the better job your attorney can do in presenting your case to the judge.

Look at the activities in the chart to help you review the role of you and your spouse as care providers for your child.

Parental Roles Chart

Activity	Parent 1	Parent 2
Attended prenatal medical visits		
Attended prenatal class		
Took time off work after child was born		
Got up with child for feedings		
Got up with child when sick at night		
Bathed child		
Put child to sleep		
Potty-trained child		
Prepared and fed meals to child		
Helped child learn numbers, letters, colors		
Helped child learn to read		
Helped child with practice for sports, dance, music		
Took time off work for child's appointments		
Stayed home from work with sick child		
Took child to doctor visits		
Went to pharmacy for child's medication		
Administered child's medication		
Took child to therapy		
Took child to optometrist		
Took child to dentist		
Took child to get haircuts		
Bought clothing for child		
Bought school supplies for child		
Transported child to school		
Picked child up after school		

Parental Roles Chart

Activity	Parent 1	Parent 2
Drove carpool for child's school		
Went to child's school activities		
Helped child with homework and projects		
Attended parent-teacher conferences		
Helped in child's classroom		
Chaperoned child's school trips and activities		
Transported child to day care		
Attended day care activities		
Transported child from day care		
Signed child up for sports, dance, music		
Bought equipment for sports, dance, music		
Transported child to sports, dance, music		
Attended sports, dance, music recitals		
Coached child's sports		
Transported child from sports, dance, music		
Knows child's friends and friends' families		
Took child to religious education or church		
Participated in child's religious education		
Obtained information and training about special needs of child		
Comforted child during times of emotional upset		

8.8 Do I have to let my spouse see the children before we are actually divorced?

Unless your children are at risk for being harmed by your spouse, your children should maintain regular contact with the other parent.

It is important for children to experience the presence of both parents in their lives, regardless of the separation of the parents. Even if there is no temporary order for parenting time, cooperate with your spouse in making reasonable arrangements for time with your children.

When safety is not an issue, if you deny contact with the other parent prior to trial, your judge is likely to question whether you have the best interest of your child at heart. Talk to your spouse or your lawyer about what parenting time schedule would be best for your children on a temporary basis.

8.9 I am seeing a therapist. Will that hurt my chances of getting custody?

If you are seeing a therapist, acknowledge yourself for getting the professional support you need. Your well-being is important to your ability to be the best parent you can be.

Discuss with your lawyer the implications of your being treated by a therapist. It may be that the condition for which you are being treated in no way affects your child or your ability to be a loving and supportive parent.

Your mental health records may be subpoenaed by the other parent's lawyer. For this reason it is important to discuss with your attorney an action plan for responding to a request to obtain records in your therapist's file. Ask your attorney to contact your therapist to alert him or her regarding how to respond to a request for your mental health records.

8.10 I am taking prescription medication to treat my depression; will this hurt my chances of getting custody?

No. Feelings of depression, anxiety, and trouble sleeping are common during a divorce. If you have any mental health concerns, seek help from a professional. Following through with the recommendations made by your health care provider will be looked favorably upon by the court, including the use of prescription medication.

8.11 Will my children be present if we go to court?

In most instances, no. Judges make every effort to protect minor children from the conflict of their parents. For this reason, most judges will not allow children to be present in the courtroom to hear the testimony of other witnesses.

Although the risk that your spouse may share information with your child cannot be eliminated, it would be highly unusual for a judge to allow a child to hear such testimony in a courtroom.

8.12 Should I hire a private detective to prove my spouse is having an affair?

It is rare to hire a private detective for this purpose. However, if custody is disputed and your spouse is having an affair, discuss with your attorney how a private investigator might help you gather evidence to support your case. Discuss the following considerations with your attorney:

- How is the affair affecting the children?
- How much will a private investigator cost?
- Will the evidence gathered help my case?

Your attorney can help you determine whether hiring a private investigator is a good idea in your particular case.

8.13 Will the fact that I had an affair during the marriage hurt my chances of getting custody?

Whether an affair will have any impact on your custody case will depend upon many factors, including:

- Whether the children were exposed to the affair
- Whether the affair had any impact on the children
- How long ago the affair occurred
- The quality of the evidence about the affair

In determining custody, a court may consider the parent's moral fitness, which includes his or her sexual activity. However, these considerations will only be taken into account if the children were exposed to sexual activity or were adversely affected by the exposure to an affair. If you had an affair during your marriage, discuss it with your attorney at the outset so that you can assess its impact, if any, on custody.

8.14 During the months it takes to get a divorce, is it okay to date or will it hurt my chances at custody?

If custody is disputed, talk with your attorney about your plans to begin dating. Your dating may be irrelevant if the children are unaware of it. However, most judges will frown upon exposing your children to a new relationship when they are still adjusting to the separation of their parents.

If your spouse is contesting custody, it may be best to focus your energy on your children, the litigation, and taking care of yourself.

If you do date and become sexually involved with your new partner, it is imperative that your children not be exposed to any sexual activity. If they are, it could harm your case for custody.

8.15   Can having a live-in partner hurt my chances of getting custody?

If you are contemplating having your partner live with you, discuss your decision with your attorney first. If you are already living with your partner, let your attorney know right away so that the potential impact on any custody ruling can be assessed.

Your living with someone who is not your spouse may have significant impact on your custody case. However, judges' opinions of the significance of this factor can vary greatly. Talk promptly and frankly with your lawyer. It will be important for you to look together at many aspects, including the following:

- How the judge assigned to your case views this situation
- Whether your living arrangement is likely to prompt a custody dispute that would not otherwise arise
- How long have you been separated from the other parent
- How long you have been in a relationship with your new partner
- The history and nature of the children's relationship with your partner
- Your future plans with your partner (such as marriage)

Living with a partner may put your custody case at risk. Consider such a decision thoughtfully, taking into account the advice of your lawyer.

8.16 I'm gay and came out to my spouse when I filed for divorce. What impact will my sexual orientation have on my case for custody or parenting time?

There are no laws in Kansas that limit your rights as a parent based upon your sexual orientation. Sexual activity by a parent, whether heterosexual or homosexual, is an insignificant factor in determining custody. However, exposing your child to sexual activity or engaging in sexual activity which harms your child are relevant factors in a custody dispute.

Your sexual orientation is not the same as your sexual activity. Be sure to choose a lawyer you are confident will fully support you in your goals as a parent. Understand that to dispel certain myths, you may need to educate your spouse, opposing counsel, and the judge.

8.17 How is *abandonment* legally defined, and how might it affect the outcome of our custody battle?

Abandonment is rarely an issue in custody litigation unless one parent has been absent from the child's life for an extended period. Under Kansas law, abandonment is determined by the facts and circumstances of each case. It must have occurred for a period of two years or more and be without a just cause or excuse. The intentional absence of a parent's presence, care, protection, and support are all considered.

Where abandonment has occurred for a period of two years or longer, a court may consider terminating parental rights as a part of a step-parent adoption, but only if doing so would be in the best interest of the child.

8.18 Can I have witnesses speak on my behalf to try to get custody of my children?

Absolutely. Witnesses are critical in every custody case. At a trial for the final determination of custody, you and the other parent will each have an opportunity to have witnesses give live testimony on your behalf.

Among those you might consider as potential witnesses in your custody case are:

- Family members
- Family friends
- Child-care providers

- Neighbors
- Teachers and coaches
- Health care providers
- Clergy members

In considering which witnesses would best support your case, your attorney may consider the following:

- What has been this witness's opportunity to observe you or the other parent, especially with your child? How frequently? How recently?
- How long has the witness known you or the other parent?
- What is the relationship of the witness to the child and the parents?
- How valuable is the knowledge that this witness has?
- Does this witness have knowledge different from that of other witnesses?
- Is the witness available and willing to testify?
- Is the witness clear in conveying information?
- Is the witness credible, that is, will the judge believe this witness?
- Does the witness have any biases or prejudices that could impact the testimony?

You and your attorney can work together to determine which witnesses will best support your case. Support your attorney by providing a list of potential witnesses together with your opinion regarding the answers to the above questions.

Give your attorney the phone numbers, addresses, and workplaces of each of your potential witnesses. This information can be critical to the role that the attorney has in interviewing the witnesses, contacting them regarding testifying, and issuing subpoenas to compel their court attendance if needed. When parents give conflicting testimony during a custody trial, the testimony of other witnesses can be helpful to determining the outcome of the case.

8.19   Will my attorney want to speak with my children?

In most cases your attorney won't ask or need to speak with your children. An exception might be where custody is disputed or where either parent has made allegations of abuse or neglect. Not all attorneys are trained in appropriate interviewing techniques for children, especially for younger children. If the attorney has not spent a lot of time with children or is not familiar with child development, the interview may not provide meaningful information. Don't hesitate to ask your attorney about his or her experience in working with children before you agree to an interview of your child.

If your attorney asks to meet with your child, provide some background information about your child first. Let your attorney know your child's personality, some of his or her interests, and any topics that might upset your child. This background will help the attorney exercise the care essential anytime a professional questions a child.

If you are concerned that going to your attorney's office for an interview will cause undue anxiety for your child, ask your attorney whether the interview can take place in a setting which would be more comfortable for your child. This might be a public place or your home.

8.20   Who is a *guardian ad litem?* Why is one appointed?

In custody cases, a *guardian ad litem* is an individual who is appointed by the court to represent the best interest of the child. The guardian *ad litem* (sometimes referred to as the *GAL*), typically an attorney, is directed by the judge to conduct an investigation on the issue of custody. Historically, guardians *ad litem* were used for this purpose. Now, it is also likely that the court will appoint an attorney for the child to advocate on the child's behalf. The role of the attorney for the child is to serve as the child's lawyer. The attorney for the child has the responsibility to represent and advocate for the child's best interest in the proceeding.

8.21   What is a *child custody expert?* Why is one appointed?

If custody is disputed, the court may order a *child custody expert* be appointed. The child custody expert is a neutral evaluator whose role is to assess the best interest of the child and to make recommendations to the court concerning custody and parenting time. The child custody expert may conduct a complete evaluation of the parties, conduct psychological testing, interview the parents and the child, and evaluate the interaction between the child and both parents. The expert is also authorized to review and receive information, records, and reports concerning all parties involved. The expert will then submit a report to the court with his or her recommendations and may testify at trial.

8.22 How might photographs or a video of my child help my custody case?

Photographs or a video depicting your child's day-to-day life can help the judge learn more about your child's needs. It can demonstrate how your child interacts with you, siblings, and other important people in your family's life. The photographs or video can portray your child's room, home, and neighborhood, as well as show your child participating in activities.

Talk to your lawyer about whether photographs or a video would be helpful in your case. Photographs are more commonly used and are typically sufficient evidence. Ask your lawyer if he or she recommends making a video, and if so, what scenes to include, the length of the video, keeping the original tapes, and the editing process.

8.23 Why might I not be awarded sole physical custody?

In Kansas, joint legal custody and joint parenting time are the presumptions. *Sole custody* is rare.

In determining physical custody and parenting arrangements, the court considers the best interest of the minor child, which may include, but are not limited to the following considerations:

- The relationship of the minor child to each parent prior to the commencement of the action or temporary hearing
- The desires and wishes of the minor child, if of an age of comprehension but regardless of chronological age, when such desires and wishes are based on sound reasoning

- The general health, welfare, and social behavior of the minor child
- Credible evidence of abuse inflicted on any family or household member.

8.24   What does it mean to be an unfit parent?

Parental unfitness means that you have a personal deficiency or incapacity which will likely prevent you from performing essential parental obligations and is likely to result in a detriment to your child's well-being.

Determinations of your fitness to be a custodial parent will largely depend upon the facts of your case. Reasons why a parent might be found to be unfit include a history of physical abuse, alcohol or drug abuse, or mental health problems which affect the ability to parent.

8.25   Does joint physical custody always mean equal time at each parent's house?

No. Joint physical custody means that each parent has continuous blocks of parenting time with the child for substantial lengths of time. However, joint physical custody does not necessarily require that each parent have equal amounts of parenting time.

8.26   If I am awarded joint physical custody, what are some examples of how the parenting might be shared?

There is no "standard" parenting time schedule. The parents are in the best position to determine and to agree on a parenting time schedule for their child. In joint physical custody arrangements, parents might choose to follow a 2-3-2 schedule, or a variation thereof, whereby one parent has the child for two weekdays, the other parent has the child for the following two weekdays, and then the child goes back to the first parent for a three day weekend. On the following page is an example parenting chart to demonstrate the 2-3-2 schedule.

2-3-2 Parenting Time Schedule

	Monday	**Tuesday**	**Wednesday**	**Thursday**	**Friday**	**Saturday**	**Sunday**
Week 1	Parent 1 at 8 A.M.	Parent 1	Parent 2 beginning at 5 P.M.	Parent 2	Parent 1 beginning at 5 P.M.	Parent 1	Parent 1
Week 2	Parent 2 at 8 A.M.	Parent 2	Parent 1 beginning at 5 P.M.	Parent 1	Parent 2 beginning at 5 P.M.	Parent 2	Parent 2

Some parents prefer to have a one week on, one week off parenting schedule. Parents should consider the age and needs and schedule of the child in determining the best schedule for the child. Typically all siblings follow the same schedule.

8.27   How is legal custody decided?

In Kansas, joint legal custody for both parents is presumed to be in the best interest of the child. Each parent awarded joint legal custody has the responsibility and authority to make all fundamental decisions regarding the child's welfare. Neither parent has a "veto" right or power over the other. Parents awarded joint legal custody are expected to co-parent and confer and jointly make the important decisions regarding their child. Examples of fundamental decisions, include, but are not limited to issues such as religion, education, and non-emergency medical treatment. You can be awarded either sole or joint legal custody.

In the rare and extraordinary circumstance that you are awarded sole legal custody, you have the sole authority to make fundamental decisions for your child, such as what school your child will attend, who your child's treating physician will be, and whether your child should undergo elective treatments or surgeries. However, even if you are awarded sole legal custody, your spouse still has the authority and responsibility to make the day-to-day or routine decisions for your child when he or she is in your spouse's care.

In almost all cases you will be awarded joint legal custody, and you and your spouse will share the decision-making authority. This necessitates that you and your spouse are able to communicate and agree upon fundamental decisions regarding your children. You and your spouse should share a mutual respect for each other, be able to communicate effectively, and be able to cooperate and work together in a co-parenting relationship.

If you share joint legal custody and are unable to reach agreement on a major decision, such as a child's school or child-care provider, you and your former spouse may be required to return to mediation or to court to resolve your dispute. This can lead to delays in decision making for matters important to your child, increased conflict, and legal fees.

8.28 How much time will our child spend with me?

Parenting time schedules vary from case to case. However, historically, a typical parenting time schedule is alternating weekends and one or two evenings during the week. Additionally, holidays are alternated between the parents and Mother's Day and Father's Day are spent with the appropriate parent. Holiday parenting time generally supersedes the regular weekly schedule for parenting time.

As in the determination of custody, the best interest of the child are what a court considers in determining the parenting time schedule. Among the factors which can impact a parenting time schedule are the past history of parenting time, the age and needs of the child, and the parents' work schedules.

If you and your spouse are willing to reach your own agreement about the parenting time schedule, you are likely to be more satisfied with it than with one imposed by a judge. Your agreed schedule is presumed by the court to be in the best interest of your child and will typically be approved by the judge. Because the two of you know your child's needs, your family traditions, and your personal preferences, you can design a plan uniquely suited to your child's best interest.

If you and your spouse are unable to reach an agreement on a parenting time schedule, either on your own or with the assistance of your lawyers or a mediator, the judge will decide the schedule.

8.29 What does it mean to have *split custody?*

Split or *divided custody* refers to a custodial arrangement whereby each parent has sole physical custody of one or more of the children. Courts generally disfavor divided custody because it separates the children from each other. However, in families with a disabled child, or a child who is in need of additional health services, the use of split custody can provide for more attention and care focused upon the child in need.

8.30   What is a *parenting plan?*

A *parenting plan* is a document detailing how you and your spouse will be parenting your child after the divorce. Among the issues addressed in a parenting plan are:

- Custody, both legal and physical
- Parenting time, including specific times for:
    - Regular school year
    - Holidays
    - Birthdays
    - Mother's Day and Father's Day
    - Summer
    - School breaks
- Phone access to the child
- Communication regarding the child
- Access to records regarding the child
- Notice regarding parenting time
- Attendance at the child's activities
- Decision making regarding the child
- Exchange of information such as addresses, phone numbers, and care providers
- Transportation of the child

Detailed parenting plans are usually better for children and parents. They increase clarity for the parents, provide security for the child in knowing what to expect, reduce conflict, and lower the risk of needing to return to court for a modification of your divorce decree.

8.31   I don't think it's safe for my children to have any contact with my spouse. How can I prove this to the judge?

Keeping your children safe is so important that this discussion with your attorney requires immediate attention. Talk with your attorney about a plan for the protection of you and your children. Options might include a protection order, supervised visitation, or certain restrictions on your spouse's parenting time, such as no overnight visitation. However, it is rare for the court to enter a no-contact order with respect to children.

Make sure you have an attorney who understands your concerns for the welfare of your children. If your attorney is not taking your worry about the safety of your children seriously, you may be better served by a lawyer with a greater understanding of the issues in your case.

Give your attorney a complete history of the facts upon which you base your belief that your children are not safe with the other parent. Although the most recent facts are often the most relevant, it is important that your attorney have a clear picture of the background as well.

Your attorney also needs information about your spouse, such as whether your spouse is or has been:

- Using alcohol or drugs
- Treated for alcohol or drug use
- Arrested, charged, or convicted of crimes of violence
- In possession of firearms
- Subject to a protection order for harassment or violence

8.32 How can I get my spouse's parenting time to be supervised?

If you are concerned about the safety of your children when they are with your spouse, talk to your lawyer. It may be that a protection order is warranted to terminate or limit contact with your children. Alternatively, it is possible to ask the judge to consider certain court orders intended to better protect your children.

Ask your attorney whether, under the facts of your case, the judge would consider any of the following court orders:

- Supervised visits
- Exchanges of the children in a public place
- Parenting class for the other parent
- Anger management or other rehabilitative program for the other parent

- A prohibition against drinking by the other parent when with the children

Judges have differing approaches to cases where children are at risk. Recognize that there are also often practical considerations, such as cost or the availability of people to supervise visits. Urge your attorney to advocate zealously for court orders to protect your children from harm by the other parent.

8.33 My spouse keeps saying he'll get custody because there were no witnesses to his abuse and I can't prove it. Is he right?

No. Most domestic violence is not witnessed by others, and judges know this.

If you have been a victim of abusive behavior by your spouse, or if you have witnessed your children as victims, your testimony is likely to be the most compelling evidence.

Be sure to tell your attorney about anyone who may have either seen your spouse's behavior or spoken to you or your children right after an abusive incident. They may be important witnesses in your custody case.

8.34 I am concerned about protecting my child from abuse by my spouse. Which types of past abuse by my spouse are important to tell my attorney?

Keeping your child safe is your top priority. So that your attorney can help you protect your child, give him or her a full history of the following:

- Hitting, kicking, pushing, shoving, or slapping your or your child
- Sexual abuse
- Threats to harm you or the child
- Threatened to abduct your child
- Destruction of property
- Torture of pets or harm to them
- Requiring your child to keep secrets
- Efforts to control you and your freedom of movement

The process of writing down past events may help you to remember other incidents of abuse that you had forgotten. Be as complete as possible.

8.35 What documents or items should I give my attorney to help prove the history of domestic violence by my spouse?

The following may be useful exhibits if your case goes to court:

- Photographs of injuries
- Photographs of damaged property
- Abusive or threatening notes, letters, or e-mails
- Abusive or threatening voice messages
- Your journal entries about abuse
- Police reports
- Medical records
- Court records
- Criminal and traffic records
- Damaged property, such as torn clothing

Tell your attorney which of these you have or are able to obtain. Ask your lawyer whether others can be acquired through a subpoena or other means.

8.36 I want to talk to my spouse about our child, but all the other parent wants to do is argue. How can I communicate without it always turning into a fight?

Because conflict is high between you and your spouse, consider the following:

- Ask your lawyer to help you obtain a court order for custody and parenting time that is specific and detailed. This lowers the amount of necessary communication between you and your spouse.
- Put as much information in writing as possible.
- Consider using e-mail or mail, especially for less urgent communication.
- Avoid criticisms of your spouse's parenting.
- Avoid telling your spouse how to parent.

- Be factual, and business-like.
- Acknowledge to your spouse the good parental qualities he or she displays, such as being concerned, attentive, or generous.
- Keep your child out of any conflicts.

By focusing on your behavior, conflict with your spouse has the potential to decrease. Additionally, talk to your attorney about developing a communication protocol to follow when communication with your spouse.

8.37 What if the child is not returned from parenting time at the agreed upon time? Should I call the police?

Calling the police should be done only as a last resort if you feel that your child is at risk for kidnapping, abuse or neglect, or if you have been advised by your attorney that such a call is warranted. The involvement of law enforcement officials in parental conflict can result in far greater trauma to a child than a late return at the end of a parenting time.

The appropriate response to a child not being returned according to a court order depends upon the circumstances. If the problem is a recurring one, talk to your attorney regarding your options. It may be that a change in the schedule would be in the best interest of your child.

Regardless of the behavior of the other parent, make every effort to keep your child out of any conflicts between the adults.

8.38 May I move out of state without the permission of the court?

No. A custodial parent must obtain the agreement of the other parent or the permission of the court prior to changing the residence of the child. If your former spouse agrees to your move, contact your attorney for preparing and submitting the necessary documents to your former spouse and the court for approval.

If your former spouse objects to your move, you must apply to the court for permission, give your spouse notice of the application, and have a court hearing for the judge to decide.

To obtain the court's permission, you must first prove that you have a legitimate reason for the move, such as a better job or a transfer of your employment. You must also prove that the move is in the best interest of your child. Temporary removal of a child in such cases is ordinarily not granted.

8.39 I am considering moving out of state. What factors will the court consider in either granting or denying my request to remove my child from Kansas?

If you are considering an out-of-state move, talk to your attorney immediately. In order to leave Kansas with your child, you must have a legitimate reason for leaving the state, such as an increased employment opportunity. The move must also be deemed by the court to be in your child's best interest. In determining your child's best interest, the court may consider many factors, including:

- The potential the move holds for increasing your child's quality of life
- The extent to which your income or employment will be enhanced
- The new living conditions and educational advantages in your new state
- The relationship between your child and each parent
- Your child's ties to Kansas

The court will also consider the impact that the move will have on the contact between your child and the other parent. Even if you have not finalized your plans to leave Kansas, seek advice from your attorney. He or she can help you gather important information that may be needed in your removal case.

8.40 After the divorce, can my spouse legally take our children out of the state during parenting time? Out of the country?

It depends upon the terms of the court order as set forth in your decree.

If you are concerned about your children being out of Kansas with the other parent, you may want some of these decree provisions regarding out-of-state travel with your child:

- Limits on the duration or distance for out-of-state travel with the child
- Notice requirements
- Information on phone numbers
- Information on physical addresses
- E-mail address contact information
- Possession of the child's passport with the court
- Posting of bond by the other parent prior to travel
- Requiring a court order for travel outside of the country

Although judges are not ordinarily concerned about short trips or vacations across state lines, you should let your attorney know if you are concerned that your child may be abducted by the other parent so that reasonable safeguards may be put in place.

8.41 What rights do I have regarding medical records and medical treatment for my child?

Usually with the presumed award of joint legal custody both parents are allowed to have access to the medical records of their children and to make emergency medical decisions.

8.42 How will I know what's going on at my child's school? What rights to records do I have there?

If you are awarded joint legal custody, you will typically have a right to have access to your child's school records.

Develop a relationship with your child's teachers and the school staff. Request to be put on the school's mailing list for all notices. Find out what is necessary for you to do to get copies of important school information and report cards. Agree with the other parent to a sharing of the "backpack" information the school may send home with your child.

Communicate with the other parent to both share and receive information about your child's progress in school. This will enable you to support your child and one another through any challenging periods of your child's education. It also enables you to share a mutual pride in your child's successes.

Regardless of the parenting time schedule, your child will benefit by your involvement in his or her education through your participation in parent-teacher conferences, attendance at school events, help with school homework, and positive communication with the other parent.

8.43 Can I still take my child to church during my parenting time?

Yes. The decision of which religion the child should be is a fundamental decision that is made by both parents. With joint legal custody, each parent retains the authority to make day-to-day decisions for the child while he or she is in their care. This means that either parent can still take their child to church or participate in religious activities during their parenting time.

8.44 What if my child does not want to go for his or her parenting time? Can my former spouse force the child to go?

If your child is resisting going with the other parent, it can first be helpful to determine the underlying reason. Consider these questions:

- What is your child's stated reason for not wanting to go?
- Does your child appear afraid, anxious, or sad?
- Do you have any concerns regarding your child's safety while with the other parent?
- Have you prepared your child for being with the other parent, speaking about the experience with enthusiasm and encouragement?
- Is it possible your child is perceiving your anxiety about the situation and is consequently having the same reaction?
- Have you provided support for your child's transition to the other home, such as completing fun activities in your home well in advance of the other parent's starting time for parenting?
- Have you spoken to the other parent about your child's behavior?
- Can you provide anything that will make your child's time with the other parent more comfortable, such as a favorite toy or blanket?

- Have you established clear routines that support your child to be ready to go with the other parent with ease, such as packing a backpack or saying good-bye to a family pet?

The reason for a child's reluctance to go with the other parent may be as simple as being sad about leaving you or as serious as being a victim of abuse in the other parent's home. It is important to look at this closely to determine the best response.

Judges treat compliance with court orders for parenting time seriously. If one parent believes that the other is intentionally interfering with parenting time or the parent-child relationship, it can result in further litigation. At the same time, you want to know that your child is safe. Talk with your attorney about the best approach in your situation.

8.45 What steps can I take to prevent my spouse from getting the children in the event of my death?

Unless the other parent is not fit to have custody, he or she will have first priority as the guardian of your child in the event of your death. All parents should have a will naming a guardian for their children. In the event you do not intend to name the other parent, talk with your attorney. Seek counsel about how to best document and preserve the evidence that will be needed to prove that the other parent is unfit to have custody in the event of your death.

9

Child Support

Whether you will be paying or receiving child support is often the subject of much worry. Will you receive enough support to take care of your children? Will you have enough money to live on after you pay child support? How will you make ends meet?

Most parents want to provide for their children. Today, the child-support laws make it possible for parents to have a better understanding of their obligation to support their children. The mechanisms for both payment and receipt of child support are more clearly defined, and help is available for collecting support if it's not paid.

The *Kansas Child Support Guidelines,* the Child Support Payment Center, and your county's District Court Trustee office all help to simplify the child-support system. As you learn more about them, matters regarding child support that appeared complex in the beginning can eventually become routine for you and the other parent.

9.1   What determines whether I will get child support?

Whether you will receive child support depends upon a number of factors. These may include how much time your child is living in your household, and each parent's ability to pay support.

If your spouse is not the biological or adoptive parent of your child, it is possible you will not receive child support from your spouse. If you have a majority of the parenting time with your child, it is likely your spouse will be ordered to pay support for any children born or adopted during your marriage.

9.2 Can I get temporary support while waiting for custody to be decided?

A judge has authority to enter a temporary order for custody and child support. This order ordinarily remains in place until a final decree is entered. A temporary support order can be entered at the time your divorce petition is filed with the court. The other parent can challenge that support order at a hearing with the court. In most cases a hearing for temporary custody and support can be held shortly after the filing of the complaint for divorce.

9.3 What is *temporary support* and how soon can I get it?

Temporary support is paid for the support of a spouse or a child. It is paid sometime after the divorce complaint is filed and continues until your final decree of divorce is entered by the court or until your case is dismissed.

If you are in need of temporary support, talk to your attorney at your first opportunity. If you and your spouse are unable to agree upon the amount of temporary support to be paid each month, talk to your attorney. If an agreement is not reached, it is likely that your attorney will file a motion for temporary support asking the judge to decide how much the support should be and when it will start.

Because there are a number of steps to getting a temporary child support order, don't delay in discussing your need for support with your lawyer. Child support will not be ordered for any period prior to the filing of a request for it with the court.

The following are the common steps in the process if a temporary support order is not obtained at the time the divorce petition is filed:

- You discuss your need for a temporary child support with your lawyer.
- Your lawyer requests a hearing date from the judge and prepares the necessary documents.
- A temporary hearing is held.
- The temporary order is signed by the judge.
- Your spouse's employer is notified to begin withholding your support from your spouse's paychecks.

- Your spouse's employer sends the support to the Kansas Child Support Payment Center (CSPC) in Topeka.
- CSPC sends the money to you.

If your spouse is not paying you support voluntarily, time is of the essence in obtaining a temporary order for support. This should be one of the first issues you discuss with your lawyer.

9.4 How soon does my spouse have to start paying support for the children?

Your spouse may begin paying you support voluntarily at any time. A temporary order for support will give you the right to collect the support if your spouse stops paying. Talk to your lawyer about obtaining temporary support and court hearings for temporary support in your county. You may have to wait several weeks before your temporary hearing can be held. It is possible that the judge will not order child support to start until the first day of the following month.

9.5 How is the amount of child support I'll receive or pay figured?

The *Kansas Child Support Guidelines* were created by the Kansas Supreme Court to provide the standards by which your child support is calculated. The guidelines are posted on the website of the Kansas Supreme Court. According to the guidelines, both parents have a duty to contribute to the support of their children in proportion to their respective gross incomes. As a result, both your income and the income of your spouse will factor into the child-support calculation.

Other factors the court may consider include:
- The additional cost of health insurance for the child
- The cost of work-related day care for the child
- Regularly paid support for other children
- Which parent claims the children as exemptions for tax purposes

Child support that is higher or lower than what the guidelines provide for may be awarded in certain cases, for example:

- When either parent or child has extraordinary medical costs
- When a child is disabled with special needs
- Whenever the application of the guidelines in an individual case would be unjust or inappropriate

When a judge orders an amount of support that is different from the guideline amount, it is referred to as a *deviation.*

Due to the complexity of calculations under the guidelines, many attorneys use computer software to calculate child support.

9.6 Will the type of custody arrangement or the amount of parenting time I have impact the amount of child support I receive?

It can. Sharing physical custody (equal parenting time) can dramatically lower child-support amounts. For this reason, it is essential that you discuss child support with your attorney prior to reaching any agreements with your spouse regarding custody or parenting time.

If you intend to mediate custody or parenting time, be sure to talk with your attorney in advance regarding how it can affect your child support.

9.7 Is overtime pay considered in the calculation of child support?

Yes, if your overtime is a routine part of your employment that you can actually expect to earn regularly. The judge can consider your work history, the degree of control you have over your overtime, and the nature of the field in which you work.

9.8 Will rental income be factored into my child support, or just my salary?

It depends. Income from other sources may be considered in determining the amount of child support. Gross income from all sources is typically used to calculate support.

9.9 My spouse has a college degree but refuses to get a job. Will the court consider this in determining the amount of child support?

The earning capacity of your spouse may be considered instead of current income. The court can look at your spouse's work history, education, skills, health, and job opportunities. The court can assign or attribute income to either parent, even an unemployed or underemployed parent.

If you believe your spouse is earning substantially less than the income she or he is capable of earning, provide your attorney with details. Ask about making a case for child support based on earning capacity or attributed income instead of actual income.

9.10 Will I get the child support directly from my spouse or from the state?

Kansas law requires that child support be withheld from the income of the payor of child support, unless there is a good reason not to have the support automatically withheld. Employers routinely withhold child support from employee wages just as they withhold taxes or retirement.

If the parent's income is not being withheld by his or her employer, the parent makes child-support payments to the Kansas Child Support Payment Center in Topeka. Payments can be made either electronically or by mail. The payment center then sends the child support to the parent receiving support. In certain cases, the parties can agree and the court can approve the direct payment of support. If this is a concern, discuss this option with your attorney.

9.11 How will I receive my child-support payment?

The Kansas Child Support Payment Center has several methods of disbursing your child-support money. The payment center can send your child-support check in the mail. However, it may take three to five business days for processing through the mail. This time frame may be even longer if it is an out-of-state check or a certified check.

You can also receive your payment by direct deposit so that your child-support payment is automatically deposited into your bank account. Additionally, your child support can be deposited directly onto an *electronic payment card,* which operates as a debit card. With the electronic payment card, your child-support payments will be transferred electronically into your card account, from which you can access your money at any automated teller machine (ATM) and is accepted anywhere debit cards are accepted. Receiving your child-support payment by direct deposit or by an electronic payment card is the fastest way to obtain your payments.

More information can be found on the Kansas Child Support Payment Center website at www.kspaycenter.com.

9.12 Is there any reason not to pay or receive payments directly to or from my spouse once the court has entered a child support order?

Yes. Once a child support order is entered by the court, the Kansas Child Support Payment Center keeps a record of all support paid. If the payment is not made through the center, the state's records will show that you are behind in your child support.

Direct payments of child support can also result in misunderstandings between parents. The payor may have intended the money to pay a child-support payment, but the parent receiving the support may have thought it was extra money to help with the child's expenses.

The payment of support through the payment center protects both parents. If a direct payment is made, be sure a written receipt is signed and filed with the clerk of the district court of the county in which your child support order was entered. This is important so that the state's records remain accurate. If no receipt is filed for a direct payment, it may later be considered a gift.

9.13 Can I go to the courthouse to pick up my child-support payment?

No. In the past, payments for child support were made to the clerk of the district court in the county where the child support-order was entered. Today, all child-support payments in Kansas are processed through a central location at the Kansas Child Support Payment Center.

9.14 How soon can I expect my child-support payments to start arriving?

A number of factors may affect the date on which you will begin receiving your child support. Here are the usual steps in the process:

- A child-support amount and start date for the support are decided either by agreement between you and your spouse or by the judge.
- Either your attorney or your spouse's attorney prepares the court order.
- The attorney who did not write the court order reviews and approves it.
- The court order is sent to the judge for signature.
- Your spouse signs a *notice to withhold income* form and delivers it to his or her employer, asking that child support be withheld from future paychecks. Alternatively, the court trustee issues an income withholding order to your spouse's employer.
- Your spouse's employer withholds the support from the paycheck.
- The child support is transferred by the employer into the Kansas Child Support Payment Center.
- The payment center sends the money to you, either by direct deposit or mail.

As you can see, there are a lot of steps in this process. Plan your budget knowing that the initial payment of child support might be delayed.

9.15 Will some amount of child support be withheld from every paycheck?

It depends upon the employer's policy and how you are paid. If support is due on the first of the month, the employer has the full month to withhold the amount ordered to be paid. If an employer issues paychecks twice a month, it is possible that half of the support will be withheld from each check and paid in to the Kansas Child Support Payment Center at the end of the month.

If an employer issues checks every other week, which is twenty-six pay periods per year, there will be some months in which a third paycheck is issued. Consequently, it is possible that no child support will be withheld from the wages paid in that third check of the month, or that some checks will be for less than 50 percent of the monthly amount due.

Example: Suppose child support is $650 per month. Payor is paid every other Friday, or twenty-six times per year. The employer may withhold $300 per paycheck for child support. Although most months the support received will be $600, for a few months it will be $900. By the end of the year, however, the payor will have paid the same amount as if $650 had been paid each month.

Over time, child-support payments typically fall into a routine schedule which makes it easier for both the payor and the recipient of support to plan their budgets.

9.16 If my spouse has income other than from an employer, is it still possible to get a court order to withhold my child support from his income?

Yes. Child support can be automatically withheld from most sources of income. These may include unemployment, worker's compensation, retirement plans, and investment income.

9.17 The person I am divorcing is not the biological parent of my child. Can I still collect child support from my spouse?

Perhaps. Your spouse may be ordered to pay child support under certain circumstances. Among the factors the court will consider is whether your spouse is acting in the role of a parent to your child.

Discuss the facts of your case in detail with your lawyer. When you are clear about what will be in the best interest of your child, your attorney can support you in developing a strategy for your case which takes into consideration not only child support but also the future relationship of your spouse with your child.

9.18   Can I collect child support from both the biological parent and the adoptive parent of my child?

When your child was adopted, the biological parent's duty to support your child ended. However, it may be possible for you to collect past-due child support from the period of time before the adoption.

9.19   What happens with child support when our children go to other parent's home for summer vacation? Is child support still due?

It depends. Whether child support is adjusted during extended parenting times with the other parent depends upon the court order in your case.

During parenting time of more than fourteen consecutive days in a month, the court may order reduced child-support payments. This is commonly referred to as an *abatement* of child support.

Before your divorce decree is entered by the court, talk with your lawyer about child-support abatement if you are anticipating that the parent paying support will have the child for an extended period.

9.20   What is a *child-support hearing officer*?

Although it is likely that your child support will be decided by the judge hearing your divorce, *child-support hearing officers* are also authorized to hear matters regarding child support. Hearing officers are attorneys who are appointed to conduct informal hearings in the same manner as a judge.

After hearing the evidence, the hearing officer will draw conclusions regarding the facts and make a decision. The judge reviews and approves the hearing officer's decision.

If you are dissatisfied with the hearing officer's decision, talk to your attorney right away about filing an appeal to the district court judge assigned to your case.

9.21   After the divorce, if I choose to live with my new partner rather than marry, can I still collect child support?

Yes. Although spousal support or maintenance (alimony) may end if you live with your partner, child support does not terminate for this reason.

9.22 Can I still collect child support if I move to another state?

Yes. A move out of state will not end your right to receive child support. However, the amount of child support could be changed if other circumstances change, such as income or costs for exercising parenting time, or for an adjustment for higher or lower cost of living.

9.23 Can I expect to continue to receive child support if I remarry?

Yes. Your child support will continue even if you remarry.

9.24 How long can I expect to receive child support?

Under Kansas law, child support is ordinarily ordered to be paid until the child dies, marries, is *emancipated* (becomes self-supporting), or reaches the age of eighteen, and has graduated from high school.

9.25 Does interest accrue on past-due child support?

Yes, interest accrues on past-due child support. The interest rate should be set forth in your decree based upon the interest rate in effect under state law on the date your decree is entered.

9.26 What can I do if my former spouse refuses to pay child support?

In most counties, the county district attorney is responsible for enforcement of child support. Some counties have attorneys who are specifically designated to perform child-support enforcement services. These attorneys are sometimes referred to as *court trustees.*

If your former spouse is not paying child support, you may take action to enforce the court order either with the help of your lawyer or the assistance of a court trustee. Unlike a private attorney, you do not pay for the services of a court trustee.

Visit the website for the district court in your county for a listing of the court trustees who can help you. The judge may order payment of both the current amount of support and an additional amount to be paid each month until the past-due child support (referred to as *arrearages*) is paid in full.

You may request that your former spouse's state and federal tax refunds be sent directly to the Kansas Child Support Payment Center. It may also be possible to garnish a checking or savings account.

Driver's licenses and certain professional licenses may also be suspended if a parent falls behind in child-support payments. However, if there is a payment plan for the payment of arrearages, then licenses will not be suspended.

Your former spouse may also be found in *contempt of court* if the failure to pay support is intentional. Possible consequences include being fined or jailed.

9.27 At what point will the state help me collect back-child support, and what methods do they use?

It depends. When the state will help you collect back-child support and the methods they will use can depend upon the amount of back-child support owed.

Driver's, recreational, and professional licenses can be suspended. State or federal income tax refunds can be intercepted. In some cases, failure to pay child support can result in a jail sentence.

You must initiate contact with the state if you want help in collecting your child support.

9.28 I live outside of Kansas. Will the money I spend on airline tickets to see my children impact my child support?

It might. If you expect to spend large sums of money for transportation in order to have parenting time with your children, talk to your attorney about how this might be taken into consideration when determining the amount of child support.

9.29 After the divorce, can my former spouse substitute buying sprees with the child for child-support payments?

No. Purchases of gifts and clothing for a child do not relieve your former spouse from an obligation to pay you child support.

9.30 Are expenses such as child care supposed to be taken out of my child support?

Perhaps. Child-care expenses are often included in child support. If the child-care expenses are included in the calculation of child support, then the parent who receives support payments from the other parent would be responsible for making the payment to the child-care provider. Alternatively, the parents could agree not to include child-care expenses in the calculation of the child support and instead agree that each parent will pay a percentage, such as 50 percent of the work- or school-related day-care expenses in addition to and separate from the child-support payment.

9.31 How does providing health insurance for my child affect my child-support amount?

If you pay the health insurance premium for your child, the amount you pay will be taken into account when calculating child support. You will receive a credit for the amount you pay per month for your child's health insurance premium.

9.32 Am I required to pay for my child's uninsured medical expenses from the child support I receive?

Yes, under the guidelines each parent is responsible for payment or reimbursement of their proportionate share of the child medical expenses that are not covered or paid by insurance, such as deductibles and co-payments. The proportionate shares of each parent are determined from their proportion of the combined incomes of both parents. For example, if one parent has income of $80,000 per year and the other parent has income of $20,000 per year, their combined income is a total of $100,000, and the parent earning $80,000 has a proportionate share of the total combined income of 80 percent and the other parent's share is 20 percent.

If there is a child medical expense, such as a $100 co-payment for a visit to the child's doctor, for example, one parent under this example would pay their proportionate share of that $100, or $80 (or 80 percent) and the other parent would be responsible for paying the remaining $20 (or 20 percent) of the doctor's $100 bill. The parents can also agree to share these child expenses equally.

9.33   Am I required to pay for the general, every day expenses for my child with the child support I receive?

Yes, if you are receiving child support, under the guidelines, you are responsible for expenses for your child such as housing, clothing, school lunches, and the cost for activities.

You will provide for your child's day-to-day expenses when the child is with you, and the other parent will pay for those expenses when the child is in their care. If you are sharing parenting time (50/50 or equal time schedule) then you may need to coordinate with the other parent for purchases of major expenses.

9.34   Can my spouse be required by the decree to pay for our child's private elementary and high school education?

Possibly. The *Kansas Child Support Guidelines* make no specific provision for private education tuition. However, some parents agree to include a provision in the decree for payment of such tuition because both of them believe it is important for their child.

If you want your spouse to share this expense for your child, talk it over with your lawyer. Be sure to provide your attorney with information regarding tuition, fees, and other expenses related to private education.

9.35   Can my spouse be required by the decree to contribute financially to our child's college education?

In Kansas the legal duty of a parent to support a child does not include payment for college education. However, if your spouse agrees to pay or to share in the payment of this expense, it can be included in the final decree and it will be an enforceable court order. Such a provision is ordinarily included in a divorce decree only as a result of a negotiated settlement.

If your decree includes a provision for payment of college education expenses, be sure it is specific. Terms to consider include:

- What expenses are included? For example, tuition, room and board, books, fees, travel.

- Is there a limit? For example, up to the level of the cost of attendance at the University of Kansas at Lawrence or a certain dollar amount.
- When is the payment due?
- For what period of time does it continue?
- Are there any limits on the type of education that will be paid for?

The greater the clarity in such a provision, the lower the risk is for misunderstanding or conflict years later.

10

Maintenance

In Kansas, spousal support is called *maintenance.* The IRS still refers to spousal support as alimony. The mere mention of the word "alimony" might stir your emotions and start your stomach churning. If your spouse has filed for divorce and is seeking maintenance, you might see it as a double injustice—your marriage is ending and you feel like you have to pay for it, too. If you are seeking spousal support, you might feel hurt and confused that your spouse is resistant to helping support you, even though you may have interrupted your career to stay home and care for your children.

Learning more about Kansas's laws on maintenance, also referred to as spousal support, can help you move from your emotional reaction to the reality of possible outcomes in your case. Uncertainty about the precise amount of maintenance that may be awarded or the number of years it might be paid is not unusual. Work closely with your lawyer. Be open to possibilities. Try looking at it from your spouse's perspective.

With the help of your lawyer, you will know the best course of action to take toward a maintenance decision you can live with after your divorce is over.

10.1 Which gets calculated first, child support or maintenance?

Maintenance. Any amount of maintenance paid or received will adjust and impact child support.

10.2   What's the difference between *spousal support* and *maintenance?*

In Kansas, maintenance and spousal support have the same meaning.

10.3   How will I know if I am eligible to receive maintenance?

Talk with your attorney about whether you are a candidate for maintenance.

The opinions of Kansas judges about awarding alimony vary greatly. Among the factors that may affect your eligibility to receive maintenance are:

- The length of your marriage
- Your contributions to the marriage, including interruption of your career for the care of children or to support your spouse's career
- Your education, work history, health, income, and earning capacity
- Your overall financial situation compared to that of your spouse
- Your need for support
- Your spouse's ability to pay support

Every case for maintenance is unique. Providing your lawyer with clear and detailed information about the facts of your marriage and current situation will allow him or her to make a maintenance assessment in your case.

10.4   What information should I provide to my attorney if I want maintenance?

If your attorney advises you that you may be a candidate for maintenance, be sure to provide complete facts about your situation, including:

- A history of the interruptions in your education or career for the benefit of your spouse, including transfers or moves due to your spouse's employment
- A history of the interruptions in your education or career for raising children, including periods during which you worked part-time
- Your complete educational background, including the dates of your schooling or training and degrees earned

- Your work history, including the names of your employers, the dates of your employment, your duties, your pay, and the reasons you left
- Any pensions or other benefits lost due to the interruption of your career for the benefit of the marriage
- Your health history, including any current diagnoses, treatments, limitations, and medications
- Your monthly living expenses, including anticipated future expenses such as health insurance and tax on maintenance
- A complete list of the debts for you and your spouse
- Income for you and your spouse, including all sources

Also include any other facts that might support your need for maintenance, such as other contributions you made to the marriage, upcoming medical treatment, or a lack of jobs in the field in which you were formerly employed.

No two maintenance cases are alike. The better the information your lawyer has about your situation, the easier it will be for him or her to assess your case for maintenance.

10.5   My spouse told me that because I had an affair during the marriage, I have no chance to get maintenance even though I quit my job and have cared for our children for many years. Is it true that I have no case?

Whereas in the past infidelity was a bar to maintenance, that is no longer the law in Kansas. Your claim for maintenance will be based upon many factors, but having an affair is not an absolute bar to getting spousal support. However, if your affair had a financial impact on the marital estate, it may be taken into consideration when determining an award of maintenance.

10.6   How is the amount of maintenance calculated?

Unlike child support, there are not specific state-mandated guidelines for determining the amount of maintenance. A judge will look at the expenses and incomes of you and your spouse, including consideration of any payments and receipts of child support.

Judges are given a lot of discretion to make their own decision on maintenance without the benefit of specific guidelines. Consequently, the outcome of a maintenance ruling by a judge can be one of the most unpredictable aspects of your divorce.

Several Kansas counties have developed non-binding guidelines for calculating maintenance.

10.7 My spouse makes a lot more money than he reports on our tax return, but he hides it. How can I prove my spouse's real income to show he can afford to pay maintenance?

Alert your attorney to your concerns. Your lawyer can then take a number of actions to determine your spouse's income with greater accuracy. They are likely to include:

- More thorough discovery
- An examination of check registers and bank deposits
- Inquiries about travel
- Depositions of third parties who have knowledge of income or spending by your spouse
- Subpoena of records of places where your spouse has made large purchases or received income
- Comparison of income claimed with expenses paid
- Inquiries of purchases made in cash

By partnering with your lawyer, you may be able to build a case to establish your spouse's actual income as greater than is shown on tax returns. If you filed joint tax returns, discuss with your lawyer any other implications of erroneous information on those returns.

10.8 I want to be sure the records on the maintenance I pay are accurate, especially for tax purposes. What's the best way to ensure this?

If you are paying child support in addition to spousal support, your maintenance payments should be made to the Kansas Child Support Payment Center in Topeka. Maintenance can be automatically withheld from your pay, just like your child support.

If you pay maintenance but no child support, make your payments through the Kansas Payment Center in Topeka, you will need your case number when making this payment.

By avoiding direct payments to your former spouse, you and he or she will have accurate records. To avoid an audit by the Internal Revenue Service, you must deduct the same amount of alimony that your spouse is reporting as income on your tax returns.

10.9 What effect does maintenance have on my taxes?

The IRS refers to maintenance as alimony. If you are required to pay maintenance according to a court order, those alimony payments are tax deductible. Likewise, if you receive maintenance according to a court order, you must pay income tax on the amount received. For more information, please see questions 14.4 through 14.6 in chapter 14.

10.10 What types of payments are considered maintenance?

Payments to a third party on behalf of your spouse under the terms of your divorce decree may be treated as maintenance. These may include payments for your spouse's medical expenses, housing costs, taxes, and tuition. These payments are treated as if they were received by your spouse then paid to the third party. Additionally, if you pay the premiums on a life insurance policy that is owned by your spouse, those payments are generally considered maintenance. Finally, if you are ordered to pay for expenses for a house owned by you and your spouse, some of your payments may be considered maintenance.

10.11 How is the purpose of maintenance different from the payment of my property settlement?

Spousal support and the division of property serve two distinct purposes, even though many of the factors for determining them are the same. The purpose of maintenance is to provide support. In contrast, the purpose of a property division is to distribute the marital assets fairly between you and your spouse.

10.12 My spouse makes a lot more money than I do. Will I be awarded alimony to make up the difference in our income?

Although the purpose of maintenance is to provide support, maintenance awards are not used to equalize the incomes of the parties. Instead, alimony may be awarded to assist the economically disadvantage spouse for a transitional period during and after the divorce, until he or she becomes economically self-sufficient. However, a disparity in income may be one factor the judge contemplates when considering an award of maintenance.

10.13 How long can I expect to receive maintenance?

In Kansas, the maximum duration of a maintenance award is 121 months (ten years) under the law. Like your right to receive maintenance, how long you will receive maintenance will depend upon the facts of your case and the judge's philosophy toward maintenance. In general, the longer your marriage, the stronger your case is for a long-term maintenance award.

You may receive only temporary maintenance, or you may receive maintenance for several years. Talk to your attorney about the facts of your case to get a clearer picture of the possible outcomes in your situation. Unless you and your spouse agree otherwise, your maintenance will terminate upon your remarriage or the death of either of you.

10.14 Does remarriage affect my maintenance?

Yes. Under Kansas law, unless your settlement agreement or divorce decree provides otherwise, maintenance ends upon the remarriage of the recipient.

10.15 Does the death of my former spouse affect my maintenance?

Yes. Under Kansas law, unless your settlement agreement or decree provides otherwise, maintenance ends upon the death of either party.

10.16 Do I have to keep paying maintenance if my former spouse is now living with a new significant other?

Yes, unless your settlement agreement or decree provides that maintenance terminates upon cohabitation. Do not stop making your maintenance payments. Instead, contact your attorney to seek a modification or termination of the maintenance award. Under certain circumstances, support may be reduced or terminated with a new court order if your former spouse is living with a new significant other.

10.17 Can I continue to collect maintenance if I move to a different state?

Yes. The duty of your former spouse to follow a court order to pay maintenance does not end simply because you move to another state, unless this is a specific provision in your settlement agreement or decree.

10.18 What can I do if my spouse stops paying maintenance?

If your spouse stops paying maintenance, see your attorney about your options for enforcing your court order. The judge may order the support be taken from a source of your spouse's income or from a financial account belonging to your spouse.

If your spouse is intentionally refusing to pay spousal support, talk to your attorney about whether pursuing a *contempt of court action* would be effective. In a contempt action, your spouse may be ordered to appear in court and provide evidence explaining why support has not been paid. Possible consequences for contempt of court include a jail sentence or a fine.

10.19 Can I return to court to modify maintenance?

It depends. Maintenance is generally not subject to modification. If your divorce decree provides that your maintenance order is "nonmodifiable," then it may not be modified. Also, your decree may not be modified to award maintenance if maintenance was not awarded in the original decree dissolving the marriage.

If maintenance is modifiable and there has been a material change in the circumstances the payor may seek to have maintenance modified or reduced. Examples include a serious illness or the loss of a job.

A request to modify maintenance for the purposes of seeking additional maintenance may not be filed if the time for payment of maintenance allowed under your original decree has already passed.

If you think you have a basis to modify your maintenance, contact your attorney at once to be sure a timely modification request is filed with the court.

11

Division of Property

You never imagined that you would face losing the house you and your spouse so happily moved into—the house where you celebrated family traditions and spent countless hours making it "home." Your spouse wants it and your lawyer says it might have to be sold.

During a divorce, you will decide whether you or your spouse will take ownership of everything from bathroom towels to the stock portfolio. Suddenly you find yourself having a strong attachment to that lamp in the family room or the painting in the hallway. Why does the collection of coins suddenly take on new meaning?

Do your best to reach agreement regarding dividing household goods. Enlist the support of your attorney in deciding which assets should be valued by an expert, such as the family business or real estate. From tax consequences to replacement value, there are many factors to consider in deciding whether to fight to keep an asset, to give it to your spouse, or to have it sold.

Like all aspects of your divorce, take one step at a time. By starting with the items most easily divided, you and your spouse can avoid paying lawyers to litigate the value of that 1980s album collection.

11.1 What system does Kansas use for dividing property?

Kansas law provides for an equitable or fair, but not necessarily equal, division of the property and debts acquired during your marriage.

137

Regardless of how title is held, the court can use its discretion to make a division of the marital assets and marital debts. In many cases this may mean an equal division, but it is also possible that as little as one-third of the assets awarded to one party and two-thirds to the other may still be considered "equitable." The court will consider a number of factors, including your debts, the economic circumstances of you and your spouse, and the history of contributions to the marriage.

11.2   What does *community property* mean?

Community property is a term used in several states which have a community-property system for dividing assets in a divorce. In states having community property laws, each spouse holds a one-half interest in most property acquired during the marriage. Because Kansas is *not* a community property state, community property laws do not apply.

11.3   How is it determined who gets the house?

One of first issues to be decided regarding the family home is the determination who will retain possession of it while the divorce is pending. Although some divorcing spouses are able to continue to live together in the same home during the divorce process, most parties prefer physical separation to provide for privacy, to establish appropriate boundaries of behavior, and to begin the transition to their separate future lives. Later, it must be decided whether the house will be sold or whether it will be awarded to you or your spouse.

Several factors to consider when determining the disposition of the home are:

- Who can afford the mortgage and expenses associated with the home
- Who has custody of the children
- Whether the house is premarital
- Whether there are other assets in the marital estate to offset the value of the home

Talk with your lawyer about your options and to consider the above factors. If you and your spouse are unable to reach agreement regarding the house, the judge will decide who keeps it or whether it will be sold.

11.4   Should I sell the house during the divorce proceedings?

Selling your home is a big decision. To help you decide what is right for you, ask yourself these questions:

- What will be the impact on my children if the home is sold?
- Can I afford to stay in the house after the divorce?
- After the divorce, will I be willing to give the house and yard the time, money, and physical energy required for its maintenance?
- Is it necessary for me to sell the house to pay a share of the equity to my spouse, or are there other options?
- Would my life be easier if I were in a smaller or simpler home?
- Would I prefer to move closer to the support of friends and family?
- What is the state of the housing market in my community?
- What are the benefits of remaining in this house?
- Can I retain the existing mortgage or will I have to refinance?
- Will I have a higher or lower interest rate if I sell the house and buy a new one?
- Can I see myself living in a different home?
- Will I have the means to acquire another home?
- If I don't retain the home and my spouse asks for it, what effect will this have on my custody case?
- Will my spouse agree to the sale of the house?
- What will be the real estate commission?
- What will be the costs of preparing the house for sale?

Selling a home is more than just a legal or financial decision. Consider what is important to you in creating your life after divorce when deciding whether to sell your home.

11.5   How do I determine how much our house is worth?

In a divorce, the value of your home can be determined a number of ways. You and your spouse can agree to the value of your home. You can seek advice from a local real estate agent on the approximate value of your home through a market analysis. Or, for a more authoritative valuation, you can hire a professional real estate appraiser to determine the value of your home. Talk to your attorney to determine the best method to value your home in your divorce.

11.6 My house is worth less than what is owed. What are my options?

Talk with your lawyer and consider consulting with a mortgage specialist. It is important to get an accurate assessment of the value of your house. Consider working with a professional, such as an appraiser or realtor, to obtain the estimated fair market value of your home.

If your house is "underwater," meaning, you owe more on the mortgage than your house is worth, you may decide to list your house for sale and keep it on the market while continuing to make your mortgage payments. Another option to consider is a short sale, where the lender accepts less money for your house than you owe. Seek advice from your lawyer and other financial experts to determine which option is best for you.

11.7 What is meant by *equity* in my home?

Regardless of who is awarded your house, the court will consider whether the spouse not receiving the house should be compensated for the equity in the house. *Equity* is the difference between the value of the home and the amount owed in mortgages against the property.

For example, if the first mortgage is $50,000 and the second mortgage from a home equity loan is $10,000, the total debt owed against the house is $60,000. If your home is valued at $100,000, the equity in your home is $40,000. (The $100,000 value less the $60,000 in mortgages equals $40,000 in equity.)

If one of the parties remains in the home, the issue of how to give the other party his or her share of the equity must be considered.

11.8 How will the equity in our house be divided?

If your home is going to be sold, the equity in the home will most likely be divided at the time of the sale, after all of the debts and the costs of the sale have been paid.

If either you or your spouse will be awarded the house, there are a number of options for the other party being compensated for his or her share of the equity in the marital home.

These could include:

- The spouse who does not receive the house receives other assets (for example, retirement funds) to compensate for their respective share of the equity.
- The person who remains in the home agrees to refinance the home at some future date and to pay the other party his or her share of the equity.
- The parties agree that the property will be sold at a future date, or upon the happening of a certain event such as the youngest child completing high school or the remarriage of the party keeping the home.

As the residence is often among the most valuable assets considered in a divorce, it is important that you and your attorney discuss the details of its disposition. These include:

- Valuation of the property
- Refinancing to remove a party from liability for the mortgage
- The dates on which certain actions should be taken, such as listing the home for sale
- The real estate agent
- Costs for preparing the home for sale
- Making mortgage payments

If you and your spouse do not agree regarding which of you will remain in the home, the court will decide who keeps it or may order the property sold.

11.9 If my spouse signs a *quitclaim deed,* does that remove his obligation to repay the mortgage?

No. A *quitclaim deed* is a legal document that transfers one person's interest in real property to another person. However, removing your spouse's name from the title of your property will not remove the obligation to repay the mortgage. You and your spouse signed a contract with the lender to repay the debt you borrowed to purchase your home. Thus, removing your spouse's name from the title on the property, does not remove the obligation to repay the mortgage. To remove your spouse from the obligation, you must seek a refinance of your current mortgage. A refinance involves obtaining a new mortgage loan to pay off the existing mortgage.

11.10 Who keeps all the household goods until the decree is signed?

The court will ordinarily not make any decisions about who keeps the household goods on a temporary basis. Most couples attempt to resolve these issues on their own rather than incur legal fees to dispute household goods on a temporary basis. However, the court may enter an order restraining the parties from transferring, selling, or destroying household goods during the divorce process, so that the goods remain intact and can be divided by the decree.

11.11 How can I reduce the risk that assets will be hidden, transferred, or destroyed by my spouse?

Consulting with an attorney before the filing of divorce can reduce the risk that assets will be hidden, transferred, or destroyed by your spouse. This is especially important if your spouse has made threats to or has a history of destroying property, incurring substantial debt, or transferring money without your knowledge.

These are among the possible actions you and your attorney can consider together:

- Placing your family heirlooms or other valuables in a safe location
- Transferring some portion of financial accounts prior to filing for divorce
- Preparing an inventory of the personal property
- Taking photographs or video of the property
- Obtaining copies of important records or statements
- Obtaining a restraining order before your spouse is served with notice of the divorce

Plans to leave the marital home should also be discussed in detail with your attorney, so that any actions taken early in your case are consistent with your ultimate goals.

Speak candidly with your lawyer about your concerns so that a plan can be developed which provides a level of protection that is appropriate to your circumstances.

11.12 How are assets such as cars, boats, and furniture divided, and when does this happen?

In most cases spouses are able to reach their own agreements about how to divide personal property, such as household furnishings and vehicles.

If you and your spouse disagree about how to divide certain items, it can be wise to consider which are truly valuable to you, financially or otherwise. Perhaps some of them can be easily replaced. Always look to see whether it is a good use of your attorney fees to argue over items of personal property. If a negotiated settlement cannot be reached, the issue of the division of your property will be made by the judge at trial.

11.13 How do I value our used personal property?

In a divorce, your personal property will be valued at its fair market value. The *fair market value* is the price a buyer would be willing to pay for the item at a garage sale or on an online auction website. For example, if you bought a sofa for $3,000 five years ago, the fair market value of the couch is what you could sell it for at a garage sale today. The fair market value is not how much the couch was when you bought it or how much it will cost to replace the couch. Instead, the value of your personal property is what you could reasonably sell it for in its current used condition.

11.14 My spouse and I own a coin collection. How will our collection be valued and divided in our divorce?

If you own a unique collection, such as a gun, art, or coin collection, talk with your attorney about how to value the collection in your divorce. It may be that you will need the collection appraised by an expert who has specialized training and knowledge to determine its value. If you and your spouse cannot agree on who will keep the collection, it is possible the judge will order the collection to be sold. The judge may also order you to divide the collection between you and your spouse.

11.15 What is meant by a *property inventory* and how detailed should mine be?

A *property inventory* is a listing of the property you own. It may also include a brief description of the property. Discuss with your attorney the level of inventory detail needed to benefit your case.

Factors to consider when creating your inventory may include:

- The extent to which you anticipate you and your spouse will disagree regarding the division of your property
- Whether you anticipate a dispute regarding the value of the property either you or your spouse is retaining
- Whether you will have continued access to the property if a later inventory is needed or whether you spouse will retain control of the property
- Whether you or your spouse are likely to disagree about which items are premarital, inherited, or gifts from someone other than your spouse

In addition to creating an inventory, your attorney may request that you prepare a list of the property that you and your spouse have already divided or a list of the items you want but your spouse has not agreed to give to you.

If you do not have continued access to your property, talk to your attorney about taking photographs or obtaining access to the property to complete your inventory.

11.16 What happens to our individual checking and savings accounts during and after the divorce?

Regardless of whose name is on the account, bank accounts may be considered marital assets and may be divided by the court. Discuss with your attorney the benefits of a temporary restraining order to protect bank accounts, how to retain access or obtain an accounting of these accounts, how to use these accounts while the case is pending, and the date on which financial accounts should be valued.

11.17 How and when are liquid assets like bank accounts and stocks divided?

Talk with your attorney early in your case about the benefits of a temporary restraining order to reduce the risk that your spouse will transfer money out of financial accounts or transfer other assets.

In many cases couples will agree to divide bank accounts equally at the outset of the case. However, this may not be advisable in your case. Discuss with your attorney whether you should keep an accounting of how you spend money used from a bank account while your divorce is in progress.

Stocks are ordinarily a part of the final agreement for the division of property and debts. If you and your spouse cannot agree on how your investments should be divided, the judge will make the decision at trial.

11.18 How is pet custody determined?

Under Kansas law, pets are considered property. There is no pet custody right similar to child custody in Kansas. However, the parties are free to agree to the disposition of their pets just as with any other property. Factors the parties may consider include:

- Who held title to the pet?
- Who provided care for the pet?
- Who will best be able to meet the pet's needs?

Some spouses agree to award the pet to one party and give the other party certain rights, such as:

- Specific periods of time to spend with the pet
- The right to care for the pet when the other person is not able to
- The right to be informed of the pet's health condition

If it is important to you to be awarded one of your family pets, discuss the matter with your attorney. It may be possible to reach a pet care agreement with your spouse that will allow you to share possession of and responsibility for your pets.

11.19 How will our property in another state be divided?

For the purposes of dividing your assets, out-of-state property is treated the same as property in Kansas. Although a Kansas court cannot order a change in the title to property located in another state, a judge can order your spouse either to turn the property over to you or to sign a deed or other document to transfer title to you.

11.20 Are all of the assets—such as property, bank accounts, and inheritances—that I had prior to my marriage still going to be mine after the divorce?

It depends. In many cases the court will allow a party to retain an asset brought into the marriage, but the following are questions the court will consider in making its determination:

- Can the premarital asset be clearly traced? For example, if you continue to own a vehicle that you brought into the marriage, it is likely that it will be awarded to you as your separate property. However, if you brought a vehicle into the marriage, sold it during the marriage, and spent the proceeds, it is less likely that the court will consider awarding you its value.

- Did you keep the property separate and titled in your name, or did you commingle it with marital assets? Premarital assets you kept separate may be more likely to be awarded to you.

- Did the other spouse contribute to the increase in the value of the premarital asset, and can the value of that increase be proven? For example, suppose one spouse owned a home prior to the marriage. After the marriage, the parties live in the home, continuing to make mortgage payments and improvements to the home. At the time of the divorce, the other spouse seeks a portion of the equity in the home. The court might consider the value of the home at the time of the marriage, any contributions to the increase in equity made by the other spouse, and the evidence of the value of those contributions.

- Do you have a prenuptial agreement? For additional explanation of this type of agreement, see question 11.36.

11.21 Will I get to keep my engagement ring?

If your engagement ring was given to you prior to your marriage, it will be considered a gift and treated as premarital property that you can keep.

11.22 What does it mean to *commingle* property?

Commingling occurs when one spouse's separate property is mixed or combined with the marital property, such that the separate property can no longer be distinguished from the marital property.

11.23 Can I keep gifts and inheritances I received during the marriage?

Similar rules apply to gifts and inheritances received during the marriage as apply to premarital assets, that is, assets you owned prior to the marriage.

Gifts that you and your spouse gave to one another may be treated as any other marital asset. For gifts received during the marriage, such as a gift from a parent, the court will need to determine whether the gift was made to one party or to both. Whether you will be entitled to keep assets you inherited, assuming they are still in existence, will depend upon the unique circumstances of your case. When dividing the marital estate, the court may consider the fact that one spouse is allowed to keep substantial nonmarital assets such as an inheritance.

The following factors increase the probability that you will be entitled to keep your inheritance:

- It has been kept separate from the marital assets, such as a separate account.
- It is titled in your name only.
- It can be clearly identified.
- It has not been commingled with marital assets.
- Your spouse has not contributed to its care, operation, or improvement.

It is less likely that you will be awarded your full inheritance if:

- It was commingled with marital assets.
- Its origin cannot be traced.

- You have placed your spouse's name on the title.
- Your spouse has contributed to the increase in the value of the value of the inheritance.

If keeping your inheritance is important to you, talk to your attorney about the information needed to build your case.

11.24 If my spouse and I can't decide who gets what, who decides? Can that person's decision be contested?

If you and your spouse cannot agree on the division of your property, the judge will make the determination after considering the evidence at your trial.

If either party is dissatisfied with the decision reached by the judge, an appeal to a higher court is possible.

11.25 How are the values of property determined?

The value of some assets, like bank accounts, is usually not disputed. The value of other assets, such as homes or personal property, is more likely to be disputed.

If your case proceeds to trial, you may give your opinion of the value of property you own. You or your spouse may also have certain property appraised by an expert. In such cases it may be necessary to have the appraiser appear at trial to give testimony regarding the appraisal and the value of the asset.

If you own substantial assets for which the value is likely to be disputed, talk to your attorney early in your case about the benefits and costs of expert witnesses.

11.26 What does *date of valuation* mean?

Because the value of assets can go up or down while a divorce is pending, it can be necessary to determine a set date for valuing the marital assets. This is referred to as the *date of valuation*. You and your spouse can agree on the date the assets should be valued. If you cannot agree, the judge will decide the date of valuation.

Among the most common dates used are the date of separation, the date of the filing of the divorce complaint, or the date of the divorce trial.

11.27 Who gets the interest from certificates of deposit, dividends from stock holdings, during the divorce proceedings?

Whether you or your spouse receives interest from these assets is decided as a part of the overall division of your property and debts.

11.28 Does each one of our financial accounts have to be divided in half if we agree to an equal division of our assets?

No. Rather than incurring the administrative challenges and expense of dividing each asset in half, you and your spouse can decide that one of you will take certain assets equal to the value of assets taken by the other spouse. If necessary, one of you can agree to make a cash payment to the other to make an equitable division.

11.29 Is my *health savings account* an asset that can be divided in the divorce?

Yes. A *health savings account (HSA)* is a tax-advantaged medical savings account to which contributions may be made by employees, employers or both. Your HSA is an asset to be included the property distribution and may be divided according to your divorce decree and transferred to another HSA. A division according to a decree does not constitute a distribution and is thus a tax-free transfer.

11.30 I worked very hard for years to support my family while my spouse completed an advanced degree. Do I have a right to any of my spouse's future earnings?

Your contributions during the marriage are a factor to be considered in both the division of the property and debts, as well as any award of maintenance. Be sure to give your attorney a complete history of your contributions to the marriage and ask about their impact on the outcome of your case.

11.31 What factors determine whether I can get a share of my spouse's business?

Many factors determine whether you will get a share of your spouse's business and in what form you might receive it.

Among the factors the court will look at are:

- Whether your spouse owned the business prior to your marriage
- Your role, if any, in operating the business or increasing its value
- The overall division of the property and debts

If you or your spouse owns a business, it is important that you work with your attorney early in your case to develop a strategy for valuing the business and making your case for how it should be treated in the division of property and debts.

11.32 My spouse and I have owned and run our own business together for many years. Can I be forced out of it?

Deciding what should happen with a family business when divorce occurs can be a challenge. Because of the risk for future conflict between you and your spouse, the value of the business is likely to be substantially decreased if you both remain owners.

In discussing your options with your lawyer, consider the following questions:

- If one spouse retains ownership of the business, are there enough other assets for the other spouse to receive a fair share of the total marital assets?
- Which spouse has the skills and experience to continue running the business?
- What would you do if you weren't working in the business?
- What is the value of the business?
- What is the market for the business if it were to be sold?
- Could you remain an employee of the business for some period of time even if you were not an owner?

You and your spouse know your business best. With the help of your lawyers, you may be able to create a settlement that can satisfy you both. If not, the judge will make the decision for you at trial.

11.33 I suspect my spouse is hiding assets, but I can't prove it. How can I protect myself if I discover later that I was right?

Ask your lawyer to include language in your divorce decree to address your concern. Insist that it include an acknowledgment by your spouse that the agreement was based upon a full and complete disclosure of your spouse's financial condition. Discuss with your lawyer a provision that allows for setting aside the agreement or for a "finders-keepers" provision if it is later discovered that assets were hidden.

An example of that type of provisions is: "The failure of one party to disclose a property interest that is subsequently discovered by the other party, shall entitle the finding party to the award of 100 percent of that undisclosed property interest, and to an award or reimbursement of that finding party's reasonable costs and attorney's fees in uncovering that property ("finders-keepers")."

This type of language in your decree or settlement agreement can allow you to pursue the award by the court to you of the entire value of such later-discovered property that was hidden from you during the divorce process. You may also have a basis for claiming that you were a victim of fraud by your spouse and receive some type of relief or additional award of property or value from the court.

11.34 My spouse and I own and operate an agricultural operation. What do I need to know about dividing our assets?

Agricultural operations can be complex because income and debts can be derived from many sources. Look for an attorney experienced in agricultural divorces and familiar with all aspects of federal programs including the *Federal Farm Bill* on federal funding for farmers. These are some of the actions that might be needed in your case:

- Sending copies of your temporary restraining order regarding property to financial institutions, sale barns, major customers, or agencies that might be involved with the transfer of the farm assets.
- Conducting more in-depth discovery in order to gather information such as the timing of payments, contracts,

agreements to withhold payment, pre-purchased feed or fertilizer, and grain delivered but not receipted, and the value and location of all assets held.

- Obtaining information under the *Freedom of Information Act (FOIA)* from federal agencies such as the Department of Agriculture or the Farm Credit Administration.

- Using a forensic accountant to help investigate, including evaluating balance sheets and tracing cash flow.

Work closely with your lawyer to be sure that you have a complete and accurate picture of your financial situation before entering settlement negotiations or proceeding to trial.

11.35 My spouse says I'm not entitled to a share of the stock options because my spouse gets to keep them only if my spouse stays employed with that company. What are my rights?

Stock options are often a very valuable asset. They are also one of the most complex issues when dividing assets during a divorce for these, among other reasons:

- Each company has its own rules about awarding and exercising stock options.

- Complete information is needed from the employer.

- There are different methods for calculating the value of stock options.

- The reasons the options were given can impact the valuation and division. For example, some are given for future performance and may be considered separate property.

- There are cost and tax considerations when options are exercised.

Rather than being awarded a portion of the stock options themselves, you are likely to receive a share of the net proceeds when the stock options are exercised.

If either you or your spouse owns stock options, begin discussing this asset with your attorney early in your case to allow sufficient time to settle the issues or to be well prepared for trial.

11.36 What is a *prenuptial agreement* and how might it affect the property settlement phase of the divorce?

A *prenuptial agreement,* sometimes referred to as a *premarital* or *antenuptial agreement,* is a contract entered into between two people prior to their marriage. It can include provisions for how assets and debts will be divided in the event the marriage is terminated, as well as provisions regarding alimony.

Your property settlement is likely to be impacted by the terms of your prenuptial agreement if the agreement is upheld as valid by the court.

11.37 Can a prenuptial agreement be contested during the divorce?

Yes. The court may consider many factors in determining whether to uphold your prenuptial agreement. Among them are:

- Whether your agreement was entered into voluntarily
- Whether your agreement was fair and reasonable at the time it was signed
- Whether you and your spouse gave a complete disclosure of your assets and debts
- Whether you and your spouse each had your own lawyer
- Whether you and your spouse each had enough time to consider the agreement

If you have a prenuptial agreement, bring a copy of it to the initial consultation with your attorney. Be sure to provide your lawyer with a detailed history of the facts and circumstances surrounding reaching and signing the agreement.

11.38 I'm Jewish and want my spouse to cooperate with obtaining a *get,* which is a divorce document under our religion. Can I get a court order for this?

Talk to your lawyer about obtaining a *get cooperation clause* in your divorce decree, including a provision regarding who should pay for it. At this time, the law regarding this has not been established in Kansas.

153

11.39 Who will get the frozen embryo of my egg and my spouse's sperm that we have stored at the health clinic?

The law on this issue is not yet established in Kansas. The terms of your contract with the clinic may impact the rights you and your spouse may have to the embryo, so provide a copy of it to your attorney for review. If permissible under your contract, you and your spouse may want to consider donating the embryo to another couple.

11.40 Will debts be considered when determining the division of the property?

Yes. The court will consider any debts incurred during the course of the marriage when dividing the property. For example, if you are awarded a car valued at $12,000, but you owe a $10,000 debt on the same vehicle, the court will take that debt into consideration in the overall division of the assets. Similarly, if one spouse agrees to pay substantial marital credit card debt, this obligation may also be considered in the final determination of the division of property and debts.

If your spouse incurred debts that you believe should be his or her sole responsibility, tell your attorney. Some debts may be considered nonmarital and treated separately from other debts incurred during the marriage. For example, if your spouse spent large sums of money on gambling or illegal drugs without your knowledge, you may be able to argue that those debts should be the sole responsibility of your spouse.

11.41 What is a *property settlement agreement?*

A *property settlement agreement* is a written document that includes all of the financial agreements you and your spouse have reached in your divorce. This may include the division of property, debts, child support, alimony, insurance, and attorney fees.

The property settlement may be a separate document, or it may be incorporated into the decree of dissolution, which is the final court order dissolving your marriage.

11.42 What happens after my spouse and I approve the property settlement agreement? Do we still have to go to court?

Not necessarily. After you and your spouse approve and sign the property settlement agreement or decree, it must still be approved by your judge. If you choose, the judge can approve your decree at a final hearing. A final hearing can be scheduled after the passing of the sixty-day mandatory waiting period after under Kansas law, assuming you and your spouse have also resolved all matters pertaining to your minor children and all support issues.

If a property settlement agreement is reached by the parties, a court date for your final hearing can often be obtained earlier than a trial date, because a final hearing requires much less time than a trial. However, a final hearing is not required. You can submit your decree to the judge for approval without you or your spouse having to go to court in most instances.

11.43 If my spouse and I think our property settlement agreement is fair, why does the judge have to approve it?

The judge has a duty to ensure that all property settlement agreements in divorces are fair, reasonable, and equitable under Kansas law. For this reason, your judge must review your agreement. The judge can consider the facts and circumstances of your case when reviewing the agreement. Not every case will result in an equal division of the assets and debts from the marriage, although this is very common.

11.44 What happens to the property distribution if one of us dies before the divorce proceedings are completed?

If your spouse dies prior to your divorce decree being entered, you will be considered married and treated as a surviving spouse under the law.

If your spouse dies within thirty days from the date your divorce decree was entered by the court, but before the decree is final, your divorce decree will generally be treated as if it were final on the date it was entered by the court.

11.45 After our divorce is final, can the property agreement be modified?

Generally, provisions in your property settlement agreement or decree dealing with the distribution of your assets and debts are not modifiable, unless both parties agree. Absent an uncommon instance of fraud, duress, or newly discovered evidence, the property settlement agreement cannot be modified by the court.

12

Benefits: Insurance, Retirement, and Pensions

During your marriage, you might have taken certain employment benefits for granted. You might not have given much thought each month to having health insurance through your spouse's work. When you find yourself in a divorce, suddenly these benefits come to the forefront of your mind.

You might also, even unconsciously, have seen your own employment retirement benefits as belonging to you and not to your spouse and referred to "my 401(k)" or "my pension." After all, you are the one who went to work every day to earn it, right?

When you divorce, some benefits arising from your spouse's employment will end, some may continue for a period of time, and others may be divided between you. Retirement funds, in particular, are often one of the valuable marital assets to be divided in a divorce.

Whether the benefits are from your employer or from your spouse's, with your attorney's help you will develop a better understanding of which benefits the law considers to be "yours" "mine," and "ours" for continuing or dividing.

12.1 Will my children continue to have health coverage through my spouse's work even though we're divorcing?

If either you or your spouse currently provides health insurance for your children, it is very likely that the court will order the insurance to remain in place until your child reaches the age of majority, or for so long as it remains available, and support is being paid for your child.

The cost of insurance for the children will be taken into consideration in determining the amount of child support to be paid.

12.2 Will I continue to have health insurance through my spouse's work after the divorce?

It depends. If your spouse currently provides health insurance for you, you may be treated as a spouse for health insurance purposes for a short period of time following the entry of your divorce decree. However, most insurance companies refuse to treat a person as a spouse after the entry of the divorce decree.

Investigate the cost of continuing on your spouse's employer-provided plans under a federal law known as *COBRA* after the expiration of your previous coverage. This coverage can be maintained for up to three years. However, the cost can be very high, so you will want to determine whether it's a realistic option. You may have other options to obtain replacement coverage.

Begin early to investigate your eligibility for coverage after the entry of the decree and your options for your future health insurance. The cost of your health care is an important factor when pursuing spousal support and planning your postdivorce budget.

12.3 What is a *QMSO*?

A *qualified medical support order (QMSO)* is a court order providing continued group health insurance coverage for a minor child. A QMSO may also enable a parent to obtain other information about the plan, without having to go through the parent who has the coverage. Rather than allowing only the parent with the insurance to be reimbursed for a claim, under a QMSO, a health insurance plan is required to reimburse directly whoever actually paid the child's medical expense. Talk with your attorney about whether a QMSO is an option for your child.

12.4   What is a *qualified domestic relations order?*

A *qualified domestic relations order (QDRO)* is a court order that requires a retirement or pension plan administrator pay you the share of your former spouse's retirement that was awarded to you in the decree. In the case of federal retirement plans, this order is called a *court order acceptable for processing (COAP).* These orders help ensure that a nonemployee spouse receives his or her share directly from the employee spouse's plan.

Obtaining a QDRO or COAP is a critical step in the divorce process. They can be complex documents, and a number of steps are required to reduce future concerns about enforcement and to fully protect your rights. These court orders must comply with numerous technical rules and be approved by the plan administrator, which is often located outside of Kansas.

Whenever possible, court orders dividing retirement plans should be entered at the same time as the decree of divorce, or as soon as possible after the entry of the decree.

12.5   How many years must I have been married before I'm eligible to receive a part of my spouse's retirement fund or pension?

To be eligible to receive a part of your spouse's retirement or pension fund, some companies require that you be married for a certain length of time. However, even if your marriage is not of long duration, you may be entitled to a portion of your spouse's retirement fund or pension accumulated during the marriage.

For example, if you were married for three years and your spouse contributed $10,000 to a 401(k) plan during the marriage, it is possible that the court would award you half of the value of the contribution when dividing your property and debts.

12.6   I contributed to my pension plan for ten years before I got married. Will my spouse get half of my entire pension?

Probably not. It is more likely the court will award your spouse only a portion of your retirement that was acquired during the marriage.

If either you or your spouse made premarital contributions to a pension or retirement plan, be sure to let your attorney know. This is information essential to determine which portion of the retirement plan should be treated as premarital and thus unlikely to be shared.

12.7 I plan to keep my same job after my divorce. Will my former spouse get half of the money I contribute to my retirement plan after my divorce?

No. Your former spouse should be entitled to a portion of your retirement accumulated only during the marriage.

Talk with your attorney so that the language of the court order ensures protection of your postdivorce retirement contributions.

12.8 Am I still entitled to a share of my spouse's retirement even though I never contributed to one during our twenty-five-year marriage?

Probably. Retirements are often the most valuable asset accumulated during a marriage. Consequently, your judge will consider the retirement along with all of the other marital assets and debts when determining a fair division.

12.9 My lawyer says I'm entitled to a share of my spouse's retirement. How can I find out how much I get and when I'm eligible to receive it?

More than one factor will determine your rights to collect from your spouse's retirement. One factor will be the terms of the court order dividing the retirement. The court order will tell you whether you are entitled to a set dollar amount, a percentage, or a fraction to be determined based upon the length of your marriage and how long your spouse continues working. For a defined benefit plan, such as a pension, the fraction used by the court to determine how much you are eligible to receive will be the number of years you were married while your spouse was employed at that company divided by the total number of years your spouse is employed with the company.

Another factor will be the terms of the retirement plan itself. Some provide for lump-sum withdrawals; others issue payments in monthly installments. Review both the terms of your court order and contact the plan administrator to obtain the clearest understanding of your rights and benefits.

12.10 If I am eligible to receive a portion of my spouse's retirement benefits, when am I eligible to begin collecting them? Do I have to be sixty-five to collect them?

It depends upon the terms of your spouse's retirement plan. In some cases it is possible to begin receiving your share at the earliest date your spouse is eligible to receive them, regardless of whether he or she elects to do so. Check the terms of your spouse's plan to learn your options.

12.11 What happens if my former spouse is old enough to receive benefits but I'm not?

Ordinarily you will be eligible to begin receiving your share of the benefits when your former spouse begins receiving his or hers. Depending upon the plan, you may be eligible to receive them sooner.

12.12 Am I entitled to *cost-of-living increases* on my share of my spouse's retirement?

It depends. If your spouse has a retirement plan that includes a provision for a *cost-of-living allowance (COLA),* talk to your lawyer about whether this can be included in the court order dividing the retirement.

12.13 What circumstances might prevent me from receiving getting part of my spouse's retirement benefits?

Some government pension plans, if they are in lieu of a Social Security benefit, are not subject to division. If you or your spouse is employed by a government agency, talk with your lawyer about whether you are entitled to any other retirement benefits and how this may affect the property settlement in your case.

12.14 Does the death of my spouse affect the pay-out of retirement benefits to me or to our children?

It depends upon both the nature of your spouse's retirement plan and the terms of the court order dividing the retirement. If you want to be eligible for survivorship benefits from your spouse's pension, discuss the issue with your attorney before your case is settled or goes to trial. He or she can advise you.

Some plans allow only a surviving spouse or former spouse to be a beneficiary. Others may allow for the naming of an alternate beneficiary, such as your children.

12.15 Can I still collect on my former spouse's Social Security benefits if he or she passes on before I do?

It depends. You may be eligible to receive benefits if:

- You were married to your spouse for ten or more years
- You are not remarried
- You are at least sixty-two-years old
- The benefit you would receive based on your own earning record is less than the benefit you would receive from your former spouse

For more information, contact your local Social Security Administration office or visit the SSA website at www.ssa.gov.

12.16 What orders might the court enter regarding life insurance?

The judge cannot order you or your spouse to maintain a life insurance policy to ensure that future support payments, such as child support and alimony are made. In most cases you will be required to pay for your own life insurance after your divorce, and you should include this as an expense in your monthly budget.

12.17 Because we share children, should I consider my spouse as a beneficiary on my life insurance?

It depends upon your intentions. If your intention is to give the money to your former spouse, by all means name the other parent as beneficiary.

However, if you intend the life insurance proceeds to be used for the benefit of your children, talk with your attorney about your options. You may consider naming a trustee to manage the life insurance proceeds on behalf of your children, and there may be reasons to choose someone other than your former spouse.

12.18 Can the court require in the decree that I be the beneficiary of my spouse's insurance policy, so long as the children are minors or indefinitely?

In Kansas, the court lacks the authority to require either party to carry life insurance for the benefit of the other. The parties are free to agree to carry life insurance and to name the other party as a beneficiary. When an agreement for life insurance is made, it is ordinarily for the purposes of ensuring payment of future support and will terminate when the support obligation has ended.

Naming you as the beneficiary on your spouse's insurance policy for purposes of ensuring payment of future child support is one option. The parties may agree to also name the children directly as beneficiaries, or require a trust be established to receive the life insurance proceeds on behalf of your children.

12.19 My spouse is in the military. What are my rights to benefits after the divorce?

As the former spouse of a military member, the types of benefits to which you may be entitled are typically determined by the number of years you were married, the number of years your spouse was in the military while you were married, and whether or not you have remarried. Be sure you obtain accurate information about these dates.

Among the benefits for which you may be eligible are:

- A portion of your spouse's military retirement pay
- A survivor benefit in the event of your spouse's death
- Health care or participation in a temporary, transitional health care program
- Ability to keep your military identification card
- Use of certain military facilities, such as the commissary

Although your divorce is pending, educate yourself about your right to future military benefits so that you can plan for your future with clarity. If your divorce is still pending, contact your base legal office, or for more information, visit the website for the branch of the military of which your spouse is or was a member.

13

Division of Debts

Throughout a marriage, most couples will have disagreements about money from time to time. You might think extra money should be spent on a family vacation, but your spouse might insist it should be saved for your retirement. You might think it's time to finally buy a new car, but your spouse thinks you driving the ten-year-old van for two more years is a better idea.

If you and your spouse had different philosophies about saving and spending during your marriage, chances are you will also have some differing opinions when dividing your debts in divorce. What you both can count on is that Kansas law provides that, to reach a fair outcome, the payment of debts must also be taken into consideration when dividing the assets from your marriage.

There are steps you can take to ensure the best outcome possible when it comes to dividing your marital debt. These include providing accurate and complete debt information to your lawyer and asking your lawyer to include provisions in your divorce decree to protect you in the future if your spouse refuses to pay his or her share.

Regardless of how the debts from your marriage are divided, know that you will gradually build your independent financial success when making a fresh start after your divorce is final.

13.1   Who is responsible for paying credit card bills and making house payments during the divorce proceedings?

In most cases, the court will not make decisions regarding the payment of credit card debt on a temporary basis. Work with your attorney and your spouse to reach a temporary agreement. Discuss the importance of making at least minimum payments on time to avoid substantial finance charges and late fees.

Often the spouse who remains in the home will be responsible for the mortgage payments, taxes, utilities, and most other ordinary expenses.

If you are concerned that you cannot afford to stay in the marital home on a temporary basis, talk with your attorney about your options prior to your temporary hearing.

13.2   What, if anything, should I be doing with the credit card companies as we go through the divorce?

If possible, it is best to obtain some separate credit prior to the divorce. This will help you establish credit in your own name and help you with necessary purchases following a separation.

Begin by obtaining a copy of your credit report from at least two of the three nationwide consumer reporting companies: Equifax, Experian, or TransUnion. The *Fair Credit Reporting Act* entitles you to a free copy of your credit report from each of these three companies every twelve months. To order your free annual report online, go to www.annualcreditreport.com, call toll-free to (877) 322-8228, or complete an Annual Credit Report Request Form and mail it to: Annual Credit Report Request Service, P.O. Box 105281, Atlanta, Georgia 30348-5281. You can print the form from the Federal Trade Commission website at www.ftc.gov/credit.

Your spouse may have incurred debt using your name. This information is important to relay to your attorney. If you and your spouse have joint credit card accounts, contact any credit card company to close the account. Do the same if your spouse is an authorized user on any of your accounts.

If you want to maintain credit with a company, ask to have a new account in your own name. Be sure to let your spouse know if you close an account he or she has been using. Be certain that any temporary orders are complied with before closing any joint account.

13.3   How is credit card debt divided?

Credit card debt will be divided as a part of the overall division of the marital property and debts. Just as in the division of property, the court considers what is equitable, or fair, in your case.

If your spouse has exclusively used a credit card for purposes that did not benefit the family, such as gambling, talk with your attorney. In most cases the court will not review a lengthy history of how you and your spouse used the credit cards, but there can be exceptions.

13.4   Am I responsible for repayment of my spouse's student loans?

It depends. If your spouse incurred student loans prior to the marriage, it is most likely that he or she will be ordered to pay that premarital debt.

If the debt was incurred during the marriage, how the funds were used may have an impact on who is ordered to pay them. For example, if your spouse borrowed $3000 during the marriage for tuition, it is likely your spouse will be ordered to pay that debt. However, if a $3000 student loan was taken out by your spouse, but $1000 of it was used for a family vacation, then the court would be more likely to order the non-tuition portion of the debt shared.

If you were a joint borrower or guarantor on your spouse's student loan and your spouse fails to pay the loan, the lender may attempt to collect from you even if your spouse has been ordered to pay the debt.

If either you or your spouse has student loan debt, be sure to give your attorney the complete history regarding the debt and ask about the most likely outcome under the facts of your case.

13.5   During the divorce proceedings, am I still responsible for debt my spouse continues to accrue?

It depends. In most cases the court will order each of the parties to be responsible for his or her own post-separation debts. In some cases, the date for dividing debt is when the parties separated households and in others, it is the date the petition for divorce was filed.

13.6   During the marriage my spouse applied for and received several credit cards without my knowledge. Am I responsible for them?

It depends. The court will consider the overall fairness of the property and debt division when deciding who should pay this debt. If your spouse bought items with the cards and intends to keep those items, it is possible that she or he will be ordered to pay the debt incurred for the purchases.

The credit card companies are unlikely to be able to pursue collection from you for the debt unless your spouse used them for the necessities of life, such as food, necessary clothing, or housing.

13.7   During our marriage, we paid off thousands of dollars of debt incurred by my spouse before we were married. Will the court take this into consideration when dividing our property and debt?

It might. Just as premarital assets can have an impact on the overall division of property and debts, so can premarital debt. Depending upon the length of the marriage, the evidence of the debt, and the amount paid, it may be a factor for the judge to consider.

Be sure to let your attorney know if either you or your spouse brought substantial debt into the marriage.

13.8   Regarding debts, what is a *hold-harmless clause*, and why should it be in the divorce decree?

A *hold-harmless provision* is intended to protect you in the event that your spouse fails to follow a court order to pay a debt after the divorce is granted. The language typically provides that your spouse shall "indemnify and hold [you] harmless from liability" on the debt.

If you and your spouse have a joint debt and your spouse fails to pay, the creditor may nevertheless attempt to collect from you. This is because the court is without power to change the creditor's rights and can make orders affecting only you and your spouse.

In the event your spouse fails to pay a court-ordered debt and the creditor attempts collection from you, the "hold-harmless" provision in your divorce decree can be used in an effort to insist that payment is made by your former spouse.

13.9 Why do my former spouse's doctors say they have a legal right to collect from me when my former spouse was ordered to pay her own medical bills?

Under Kansas law, you could be held liable for the "necessities of life" of your spouse, such as health care, although this is rare. Your divorce decree or settlement agreement does not take away the legal rights of creditors to collect debts. Contact your attorney about your rights to enforce the court order that your spouse pay his or her own medical bills.

13.10 My spouse and I have agreed that I will keep our home; why must I refinance the mortgage?

There may be a number of reasons why your spouse is asking you to refinance the mortgage. First, the mortgage company cannot be forced to take your spouse's name off of the mortgage note. This means that if you did not make the house payments, the lender could pursue collection against your spouse.

Second, your spouse may want to receive their share of the home equity. It may be possible for you to borrow additional money at the time of refinancing to pay your spouse his or her share of the equity in the home.

Third, the mortgage on your family home may prevent your spouse from buying a home in the future. Because there remains a risk that your spouse could be pursued for the debt to the mortgage company, it is unlikely that a second lender will want to take the risk of extending further credit to your spouse.

13.11 Can I file for bankruptcy while my divorce is pending?

Yes. Consult with your attorney if you are considering filing for bankruptcy while your divorce is pending. It will be important for you to ask yourself a number of questions, such as:

- Should I file for bankruptcy on my own or with my spouse?
- How will filing for bankruptcy affect my ability to purchase a home in the future?
- Which debts can be discharged in bankruptcy, and which cannot?
- How will a bankruptcy affect the division of property and debts in the divorce?
- How might a delay in the divorce proceeding due to a bankruptcy impact my case?
- What form of bankruptcy is best for my situation?

If you use a different attorney for your bankruptcy than you have for your divorce, be sure that each attorney is kept fully informed about the developments in the other case.

13.12 What happens if my spouse files for bankruptcy during our divorce?

Contact your attorney right away. The filing of a bankruptcy while your divorce is pending can have a significant impact on your divorce. Your attorney can advise you whether certain debts are likely to be discharged in the bankruptcy, the delay a bankruptcy may cause to your divorce, and whether bankruptcy is an appropriate option for you.

13.13 Can I file for divorce while I am in bankruptcy?

Yes, however, you must receive the bankruptcy court's permission to proceed with the divorce. Although in bankruptcy, your property is protected from debt collection by the "automatic stay." The stay can also prevent the divorce court from dividing property between you and your spouse until you obtain the bankruptcy court's permission to proceed with the divorce.

13.14 What should I do if my former spouse files for bankruptcy after our divorce?

Contact your attorney immediately. If you learn that your former spouse has filed for bankruptcy, you may have certain rights to object to the discharge of any debts your spouse was ordered to pay under your divorce decree. If you fail to take action, it is possible that you will be held responsible for debts your spouse was ordered to pay.

13.15 If I am awarded child support or alimony in my decree, can these obligations be discharged if my former spouse files for bankruptcy after our divorce?

No, support obligations such as child support and alimony are not dischargeable in bankruptcy, meaning these debts cannot be eliminated in a bankruptcy proceeding.

13.16 What happens if my former spouse does not pay their obligations in the decree?

If your former spouse does not pay the debts assigned to him or her in the decree, you may be able to pursue a *contempt of court* action. A party is in contempt of court if they willfully disobey or disregard a court order. Talk with your attorney to determine whether a contempt of court action may be filed in your case to enforce your rights under your decree.

14

Taxes

Nobody likes a surprise letter from the Internal Revenue Service saying he or she owes more taxes. When your divorce is over, you want to be sure that you don't later discover you owe taxes you weren't expecting to pay.

A number of tax issues may arise in your divorce. Your attorney may not be able to answer all of your tax questions, so consulting your accountant or tax advisor for additional advice might be necessary.

Taxes are important considerations in both settlement negotiations and trial preparation. They should not be overlooked. Taxes can impact many of your decisions, including those regarding alimony, division of property, and the receipt of benefits.

Be sure to ask the professionals helping you about the tax implications in your divorce so you don't get that letter in the mail that begins, "Dear Taxpayer:…"

14.1 Will either my spouse or I have to pay income tax when we transfer property or pay a property settlement to one another according to our divorce decree?

No. However, it is important that you see the future tax consequences of a subsequent withdrawal, sale, or transfer of certain assets you receive in your divorce.

It is important to ask your attorney to take tax consequences into consideration when looking at the division of your assets.

14.2   Is the amount of child support I pay tax deductible?

No.

14.3   Do I have to pay income tax on any child support I receive?

No. Your child support is tax free regardless of when it is paid or when it is received.

14.4   What does the IRS consider alimony?

Amounts paid under a divorce decree or according to a written separation agreement entered into between you and your spouse will be considered alimony if:

- You and your spouse or former spouse do not file a joint return with each other
- The payment is in cash (including checks or money orders)
- The payment is received by (or on behalf of) your spouse or former spouse
- You and your former spouse are not members of the same household when you make the payment
- You have no liability to make the payment (in cash or property) after the death of your spouse or former spouse
- Your payment is not treated as child support or a property settlement.

Therefore, not all payments made according to a divorce or separation decree are alimony. Alimony does not include:

- Child support
- Noncash property settlements
- Payments to keep up the taxpayer's property
- Use of the payor's property

14.5   Is the amount of alimony I am ordered to pay tax deductible?

Yes. Spousal support paid according to a court order is deductible. This will include court-ordered maintenance or alimony and may also include other forms of support provided to your former spouse (but not child support). Your tax deduction is a factor to consider when determining a fair amount of alimony to be paid in your case.

14.6   Do I have to pay tax on the alimony I receive?

Yes. You must pay income tax on the spousal support you receive. In Kansas, spousal support is known as "maintenance". This will include court-ordered maintenance and may also include other forms of spousal support, but not child support, paid by your spouse.

Income tax is a critical factor in determining a fair amount of alimony. Insist that your attorney bring this issue to the attention of your spouse's lawyer, or to the judge, if your case proceeds to trial, so that both the tax you pay and the deduction your spouse receives are taken into consideration.

Be sure to consult with your tax advisor about payment of tax on your spousal support. Making estimated tax payments throughout the year or withholding additional taxes from your wages can avoid a burdensome tax liability at the end of the year.

It is important to budget for payment of tax on your alimony. Taxes are also another item to consider when looking at your monthly living expenses for the purposes of seeking an maintenance award.

14.7   Is there anything else I should know about alimony and taxes?

If your alimony payments to your spouse decrease or end during the first three calendar years after your divorce, you may be subject to the IRS *recapture rule.* You are subject to the recapture rule if the alimony you pay in the third year decreases by more than $15,000 from the second year or alimony you pay in the second and third year decreases significantly from the alimony you pay in the first year.

If you are subject to this rule, you must claim a portion of the alimony payments you've previously deducted as income in the third year. Likewise, the recipient can deduct part of the alimony payments he or she previously claimed as income in the third year. This recapture rule is complicated and you should consult with your accountant or tax advisor prior to reaching any settlement on the payment of alimony.

14.8 During the divorce proceedings, is our tax filing status affected?

It can be. You are considered unmarried if your decree is final by December 31 of the tax year.

If you are considered unmarried, your filing status is either "single" or, under certain circumstances, "head of household." If your decree is not final as of December 31, your filing status is either "married filing a joint return" or "married filing a separate return," unless you live apart from your spouse and meet the exception for "head of household."

While your divorce is in progress, talk to both your tax advisor and your attorney about your filing status. It may be beneficial to figure your tax on both a joint return and a separate return to see which gives you the lower tax. IRS Publication 504, Divorced or Separated Individuals, provides more detail on tax issues while you are going through a divorce.

14.9 Should I file a joint income tax return with my spouse while our divorce is pending?

Consult your attorney and your tax advisor to determine the risks and benefits of filing a joint return with your spouse. Compare this with the consequences of filing your tax return separately. Often the overall tax liability will be less with the filing of a joint return, but other factors are important to consider.

When deciding whether to file a joint return with your spouse, consider any concerns you have about the accuracy and truthfulness of the information on the tax return. If you have any doubts, consult both your attorney and your tax advisor before agreeing to sign a joint tax return with your spouse. Prior to filing a return with your spouse, try to reach agreement about how any tax owed or refund expected will be shared, and ask your lawyer to assist you in getting this in writing.

14.10 My spouse will not cooperate in providing the necessary documents to prepare or file our taxes jointly. What options do I have?

Talk with your attorney about requesting your spouse cooperate in the preparation and filing of your joint return.

Although a judge cannot order your spouse to sign a joint return, he or she can penalize them for their unreasonable refusal to do so.

14.11 For tax purposes, is one time of year better to divorce than another?

It depends upon your tax situation. If you and your spouse agree that it would be beneficial to file joint tax returns for the year in which you are divorcing, you may wish to not have your divorce finalized before the end of the year.

Your marital status for filing income taxes is determined by your status on December 31. Consequently, if you both want to preserve your right to file a joint return, your decree should not be entered before December 31 of that year.

14.12 What tax consequences should I consider regarding the sale of our home?

When your home is sold, whether during your divorce or after, the sale may be subject to a *capital gains tax*. If your home was your primary residence and you lived in the home for two of the preceding five years, you may be eligible to exclude up to $250,000 of the gain on the sale of your home. If both you and your spouse meet the ownership and residence tests, you may be eligible to exclude up to $500,000 of the gain.

If you anticipate the gain on the sale of your residence to be over $250,000, talk with your attorney early in the divorce process about a plan to minimize the tax liability. For more information, see IRS Publication 523, Selling Your Home, or visit the IRS website at www.irs.gov and talk with your tax advisor.

14.13 How might capital gains tax be a problem for me years after the divorce?

Future capital gains tax on the sale of property should be discussed with both your attorney and your tax advisor during the negotiation and trial preparation stages of your case. This is especially important if the sale of the property is imminent. Failure to do so may result in an unfair outcome.

For example, suppose you agree that your spouse will be awarded the proceeds from the sale of your home valued at

$200,000, after the real estate commission, and you will take the stock portfolio also valued at $200,000.

Suppose that after the divorce, you decide to sell the stock. It is still valued at $200,000, but you learn that its original price was $120,000 and that you must pay capital gains tax of 15 percent on the $80,000 of gain. You pay tax of $12,000, leaving you with $188,000.

Meanwhile, your former spouse sells the marital home but pays no capital gains tax because he qualifies for the $250,000 exemption. He is left with the full $200,000.

Tax implications of your property division should always be discussed with your attorney, with support from your tax advisor as needed.

14.14 During and after the divorce, who gets to claim the children as dependents?

This issue should be addressed in settlement negotiations or at trial, if settlement is not reached.

The judge has discretion to determine which parent will be entitled to claim the children as exemptions for income tax purposes. Where child support has been ordered according to the *Kansas Child Support Guidelines,* some judges order that the exemptions be shared or alternated.

However, most judges will order that the payor of child support be current on his or her child support obligation to be eligible to claim the income tax dependency exemption. Additionally, if one party has income so low or so high that he or she will not benefit from the dependency exemption, the court may award the exemption to the other parent.

14.15 My decree says I have to sign IRS Form 8332 so my former spouse can claim our child as an exemption, because I have custody. Should I sign it once for all future years?

No. Child custody and child support can be modified in the future. If there is a future modification of custody or support, which parent is entitled to claim your child as an exemption could change. The best practice is to provide your former spouse a timely copy of Form 8332 signed by you for the appropriate tax year only.

14.16   Can my spouse and I split the child-care tax credit?

According to the *Kansas Child Support Guidelines,* the value of the federal income tax credit for child care must be considered when determining the payor spouse's obligation to contribute to child-care expenses.

The value of the federal child-care tax credit must be subtracted from the actual costs of child care to arrive at a figure for net child-care expenses owed by the spouse paying support.

Only the custodial parent is allowed to claim the credit. If you are a noncustodial parent and paying child care, talk to your lawyer about how to address this issue in your divorce decree.

14.17   Do I have to pay taxes on the portion of my spouse's 401(k) that was awarded to me in the divorce?

If you have been awarded a portion of your former spouse's 401(k) or 403(b) retirement plan, any distribution of these funds to you will be subject to regular income tax. However, it may be possible for you to elect to receive all or a portion of these assets without incurring the 10 percent early withdrawal penalty (applicable if you are under age fifty-nine and one-half) if you decide to take the money rather than keeping an account in your name or rolling over the assets to an IRA or other permitted retirement account. Talk with your attorney and your tax advisor to determine your options.

14.18   Is the cost of getting a divorce, including my attorney fees, tax deductible under any circumstances?

Your legal fees for getting a divorce are not deductible. However, a portion of your attorney fees may be deductible if they are for:

- The collection of sums included in your gross income, such as alimony or interest income
- Advice regarding the determination of taxes or tax due.

Attorney fees are "miscellaneous" deductions for individuals and are consequently limited to 2 percent of your adjusted gross income. More details can be found in IRS Publication 529, Miscellaneous Deductions.

You may also be able to deduct fees you pay to appraisers or accountants who help. Talk to your tax advisor about whether any portion of your attorney fees or other expenses from your divorce is deductible.

14.19 Do I have to complete a new Form W-4 for my employer because of my divorce?

Completing a new Form W-4 Employee's Withholding Certificate, will help you to claim the proper withholding allowances based upon your marital status and exemptions. Also, if you are receiving alimony, you may need to make quarterly estimated tax payments. Consult with your tax advisor to ensure you are making the most preferable tax planning decision.

14.20 What is *innocent spouse relief* and how can it help me?

Innocent spouse relief refers to a method of obtaining relief from the Internal Revenue Service for taxes owed as a result of a joint income tax return filed during your marriage. Numerous factors affect your eligibility for innocent spouse tax relief, such as:

- You would suffer a financial hardship if you were required to pay the tax.
- You did not significantly benefit from the unpaid taxes.
- Your suffered abuse during your marriage.
- You thought your spouse would pay the taxes on the original return.

Talk with both your attorney and your tax advisor if you are concerned about liability for taxes arising from joint tax returns filed during the marriage. You may benefit from a referral to an attorney who specializes in tax law.

15

Going to Court

Most divorce cases settle and a trial is not necessary. However, for those who cannot settle, a court hearing will be required to obtain a divorce and a resolution of your issues.

For many of us, our images of going to court are created by movie scenes and our favorite television shows. We picture the witness breaking down in tears after a grueling cross-examination. We see lawyers moving around the courtroom, waving their arms as they plead their case to the jury.

Hollywood drama, however, is a far cry from reality. Going to court for your divorce can mean many things, ranging from sitting in a hallway while waiting for the lawyers and judges to conclude a conference, to being on the witness stand giving mundane answers to questions about your monthly living expenses.

Regardless of the nature of your court proceeding, going to court often evokes a sense of anxiety. Perhaps your divorce might be the first time in your life that you have even been in a courtroom. Be assured that these feelings of nervousness and uncertainty are normal.

Understanding what will occur in court and being well prepared for any court hearings will relieve much of your stress. Knowing the order of events, the role of the people in the courtroom, etiquette in the courtroom, and what is expected of you will make the entire experience easier.

Your lawyer will be with you at all times to support you any time you go to court. Remember, every court appearance moves you one step closer to completing your divorce so that you can move forward with your life.

15.1 What do I need to know about appearing in court and court dates in general?

Court dates are important. As soon as you receive a notice from your attorney about a court date in your case, confirm whether your attendance will be required and put it on your calendar.

Ask your attorney about the nature of the hearing, including whether the judge will be listening to testimony by witnesses, or merely listening to the arguments of the lawyers.

Ask whether it is necessary for you to meet with your attorney or take any other action to prepare for the hearing, such as providing additional information or documents.

Find out how long the hearing is expected to last. It may be as short as a few minutes or as long as a day or more.

If you plan to attend the hearing, determine where and when to meet your attorney. Depending upon the type of hearing, your lawyer may want you to arrive in advance of the scheduled hearing time to prepare.

Make sure you know the location of the courthouse, where to park, and the floor and room number of the courtroom. Planning for such simple matters as change for a parking meter can eliminate unnecessary stress. If you want someone to go to court with you to provide you support, check with your attorney first.

15.2 When and how often will I need to go to court?

Whether and how often you will need to go to court will depend upon a number of factors. Depending upon the complexity of your case, you may have only one hearing or numerous court hearings throughout the course of your divorce.

Some hearings, usually those on procedural matters, are attended only by the attorneys. These could include requests for the other side to provide information or for the setting of certain deadlines. These hearings are often brief and held in the judge's chambers rather than in the courtroom. Other hearings, such as temporary hearings for custody or support, are typically attended by both parties and their attorneys. Still others may be by conference call with the attorneys and the judge.

If you and your spouse settle all of the issues in your case, although not required, you can choose to testify at a final hearing in which the judge will review and approve your decree.

If your case proceeds to trial, your appearance will be required for the duration of the trial. In Kansas, divorce matters are heard before a judge only; juries do not hear divorces.

15.3 How much notice will I receive about appearing in court?

The amount of notice you will receive for any court hearing can vary from a few days to several weeks. Ask your attorney whether and when it will be necessary for you to appear in court on your case so that you can have ease in preparing and planning.

If you receive a notice of a hearing, contact your attorney immediately. He or she can tell you whether your appearance is required and what other steps are needed to prepare.

15.4 I am afraid to be alone in the same room with my spouse. When I go to court, is this going to happen if the lawyers go into the judge's office to discuss the case?

Talk to your lawyer. Prior to any court hearing, you and your spouse may be asked to wait while your attorneys meet with the judge to discuss preliminary matters.

A number of options are likely to be available to ensure that you feel safe. These might include having you or your spouse wait in different locations or having a friend or family member present, or for you to wait outside the courtroom.

Your lawyer wants to support you in feeling secure throughout all court proceedings. Just let him or her know your concerns.

15.5 Do I have to go to court every time there is a court hearing on any motion?

Not necessarily. Some matters will be decided by the judge after listening to the arguments of the lawyers. These hearings are sometimes held in the judge's office, referred to as *chambers,* or sometimes by telephone, and you will not be required to attend.

15.6 My spouse's lawyer keeps asking for *continuances of court dates.* Is there anything I can do to stop this?

Continuances of court dates are not unusual in divorces. A court date might be postponed for many reasons, including a conflict on the calendar of one of the attorneys or the judge, the lack of availability of one of the parties or an important witness, or the need for more time to prepare.

Discuss with your attorney your desire to move your case forward without further delay, so that repeated requests for continuances can be resisted.

15.7 If I have to go to court, will I be put on the witness stand? Will there be a jury?

In Kansas, divorce matters are heard before a judge only; juries do not hear divorces. Whether you will be put on the stand will depend upon the nature of the issues in dispute, the judge assigned to your case, and your attorney's strategy for your case.

15.8 My lawyer said I need to be in court for our temporary hearing next week. What's going to happen?

A temporary hearing is held to determine such preliminary matters as who remains in the house while your divorce is pending, temporary custody, temporary support, and other financial matters. The procedure for your temporary hearing can vary depending upon the county in which your case was filed, the judge to which the case is assigned, and whether temporary custody is disputed.

Most temporary hearings are held on the basis of written affidavits and the arguments of the lawyers. While you should plan to attend your temporary hearing, it is possible that the hearing will be held in the judge's chambers with only the judge and attorneys present.

Even if your temporary hearing is held in the judge's chambers, your presence at the hearing is still important. Your attorney may need additional information from you during the hearing, and last-minute negotiations at the courthouse to resolve temporary issues are not uncommon.

In some counties, your hearing will be one of numerous other hearings on the judge's calendar. You may find yourself in a courtroom with many other lawyers and their clients, all having matters scheduled before the court that day. Even though you are present in the courtroom, your attorney will make your argument to the judge and it is unlikely you will be required to provide formal testimony.

If temporary custody is disputed, you and other witnesses might be required to take the witness stand to give testimony at your temporary hearing. If this is the case, meeting with your attorney in advance to fully prepare is very important. Talk to your lawyer about the procedure you should expect for the temporary hearing in your case.

15.9 Do I have to go to court if all of the issues in my case are settled?

No. If you and your spouse settle all of the issues in your case resulting in a written settlement agreement, you are typically not required to testify in court. Some counties may require a final hearing even if a written agreement has been reached on all issues, particularly if one party or both are not represented by an attorney.

A final hearing is a brief hearing in which your attorney or the judge will ask you and your spouse questions relating to the agreements you and your spouse reached. At this hearing, the judge will review and approve your decree and may ask you several questions about the contents of the decree as well.

15.10 Are there any rules about courtroom etiquette that I need to know?

Knowing a few tips about being in the courtroom will make your experience easier.

- Dress appropriately. Avoid being a distraction with overly casual dress, lots of jewelry, revealing clothing, or extreme hairstyles
- Don't bring beverages into the courtroom. Most courts have rules which do not allow food and drink in courtrooms. If you need water, ask your lawyer.

- Dispose of chewing gum before giving testimony.
- Don't talk out loud in the courtroom unless you're on the witness stand or being questioned by the judge. In many courtrooms there are sensitive microphones that may pick up even your whispering.
- Do not enter the judge's office.
- Stand up whenever the judge is entering or leaving the courtroom.
- Be sure to turn off all of your electronic devices, especially cellular phones.
- Be mindful that the judge may be observing you and those you bring to the hearing at all times.

Although you may feel anxious initially, you'll likely feel more relaxed about the courtroom setting once your hearing gets underway.

15.11 What is the role of the *court clerk?*

The *court clerk* or *judicial assistant* provides support for the judge and lawyers in the management of the court calendar and the courtroom. He or she assists in the scheduling of court hearings and the management of legal documents given to the judge for review, such as temporary orders and divorce decrees.

15.12 Will there be a *court reporter,* and what will he or she do?

A *court reporter* is a professional trained to make an accurate record of the words spoken and documents offered into evidence during court proceedings. Some counties use electronic recording devices rather than court reporters.

A written transcript of a court proceeding may be purchased from the court reporter or made from the digital reading. If your case is appealed, the transcript prepared by the court reporter will be used by the appeals court to review the facts of your case.

The court reporter is sometimes also responsible for managing documents and other items offered into evidence at trial.

Some hearings are held "off the record," which means that the court reporter is not making a record of what is being said. Ordinarily these are matters for which no appeal is expected to be taken.

15.13 Will I be able to talk to my attorney while we are in court?

During court proceedings it is important that your attorney give his or her attention to anything being said by the judge, witnesses, or your spouse's lawyer. For this reason, your attorney will avoid talking with you when anyone else in the courtroom is speaking.

Plan to have pen and paper with you when you go to court. If your court proceeding is underway and your lawyer is listening to what is being said by others in the courtroom, write him or her a note with your questions or comments.

It is critical that your attorney hear each question asked by the other lawyer and all answers given by each witness. If not, opportunities for making objections to inappropriate evidence may be lost. You can support your attorney in doing an effective job for you by avoiding talking to him or her while a court hearing is in progress.

If your court hearing is lengthy, breaks will be taken. You can use this time to discuss with your attorney any questions or observations you have about the proceeding.

15.14 What questions might my lawyer ask me at about the problems in our marriage and why I want the divorce?

Because Kansas is a "no-fault" state, your lawyer will ask you questions to show the court that the marriage is irretrievably broken due to "irreconcilable differences", without going into detail about the specific difficulties in your marriage.

The questions might be similar to these:

Attorney: "Have differences arisen during the course of your marriage?"

You: "Yes."

Attorney: "Have you and your spouse made efforts to reconcile those differences?"

You: "Yes"

Attorney: "Have your efforts at reconciliation been successful?"

You: "No."

Attorney: "Do you believe further efforts at reconciliation would be beneficial?"

You: "No."

Attorney: "In your opinion, is your marriage irretrievably broken?"

You: "Yes."

If your spouse disagrees, he or she may give the opinion that the marriage can be saved. However, most judges recognize that it takes two willing partners for a marriage to be reconciled.

It is unlikely that you will be asked in great detail about the nature of the marital problems that led to the divorce. In the majority of cases, questions like those above will satisfy the judge that the requirements under Kansas law for the dissolving of a marriage have been met.

15.15 My lawyer said that the judge has issued a *pretrial order* having to do with my upcoming trial and that we'll have to comply with it. What does this mean?

Ask your lawyer for a copy of the *pretrial order*. Some judges will order that certain information be provided either to the opposing party or to the judge in advance of trial. This might include:

- A list of issues that have been settled
- A list of issues that are still disputed
- Agreements, referred to as *stipulations,* as to the truth of certain facts
- The names of witnesses.
- Exhibits
- A summary of how you want the judge to decide the case
- Deadlines are given for providing the information.

15.16 What is a *pretrial conference?*

A *pretrial conference* is a meeting held with the lawyers and the judge to review information related to an upcoming trial, such as:

- How long the trial is expected to last
- The issues in dispute
- The law surrounding the disputed issues
- The identification of witnesses
- Trial exhibits
- The status of negotiations and whether mediation might be helpful, if not previously attempted.

Often the trial date is set at the pretrial conference. If a pretrial conference is held in your case, ask your attorney whether you should attend. In many counties the parties' attendance is required. Your attorney may request that you either be present for the conference or be available by phone.

15.17 Besides meeting with my lawyer, is there anything else I should do to prepare for my upcoming trial?

Yes. Be sure to review your deposition and any information you provided in your discovery, such as answers to interrogatories. Also be sure to review any affidavits previously submitted to the judge, such as your financial affidavit prepared for your temporary hearing. At trial, it is possible that you will be asked some of the same questions. If you think you might give different answers at trial, discuss this with your lawyer. It is important that your attorney know in advance of trial whether any information you provided during the discovery process has changed.

15.18 I'm meeting with my lawyer to prepare for trial. How do I make the most of these meetings?

Meeting with your lawyer to prepare for your trial is important to achieving a good outcome. Come to the meeting prepared to discuss the following:

- The issues in your case
- Your desired outcome on each of the issues
- The questions you might be asked at trial by both lawyers
- The exhibits that will be offered into evidence during the trial

- The witnesses for your trial
- The status of negotiations

Your meeting with your lawyer will help you better understand what to expect at your trial and make the trial experience easier.

15.19 My lawyer says that the law firm is busy with trial preparation. What exactly is my lawyer doing to prepare for my trial?

Countless tasks are necessary to perform to prepare your case for trial. Some begin very early in your case while other tasks are done all through the case. These are just some of them:

- Developing arguments to be made on each of the contested issues
- Researching and reviewing the relevant law in your case
- Reviewing the facts of your case to determine which witnesses are best suited to testifying about them
- Reviewing, selecting, and preparing exhibits
- Preparing questions for all witnesses
- Preparing any pretrial motions or briefs
- Preparing an opening statement and closing statement
- Reviewing rules on evidence to prepare for any objections to made or opposed at trial
- Determining the order of witnesses and all exhibits
- Preparing your file for the day in court, including preparing a trial notebook with essential information

Your lawyer is committed to a good outcome for you in your divorce. He or she will be engaged in many important actions to fully prepare your case for trial. Experience has shown that careful and extensive preparation for trial is necessary for a successful outcome.

15.20 How do I know who my witnesses will be at trial?

Well in advance of your trial date, your lawyer will discuss with you whether other witnesses, besides you and your spouse, will be necessary. Witnesses can include family members, friends, child-care providers, or clergy members. When thinking of potential witnesses, consider your relationship with the witness, whether that witness has had an opportunity to observe relevant facts, and whether the witness has knowledge different from that of other witnesses. For more information on identifying potential witnesses, please see question 8.18 in chapter 8.

You may also have expert witnesses testify on your behalf. An expert witness will provide opinion testimony based upon specialized knowledge, training, or experience. For example, a psychologist, real estate appraiser, or accountant may provide expert testimony on your behalf.

15.21 My divorce is scheduled for trial. Does this mean there is no hope for a settlement?

Many cases are settled after a trial date is set. The setting of a trial date may cause you and your spouse to think about the risks and costs of going to trial. This can help you and your spouse focus on what is most important to you and lead you toward a negotiated settlement. Because the costs of preparing for and proceeding to trial are substantial, it is best to engage in settlement negotiations well in advance of your trial date. However, it is not uncommon for cases to settle a few days before trial, or even at the courthouse before or after your trial begins.

15.22 Can I prevent my spouse from being in the courtroom?

Probably not. Because your spouse has a legal interest in the outcome of your divorce, he or she has a right to be present. Kansas courtrooms are generally open to the public. Consequently, it is not uncommon for persons not involved in your divorce to pass through the courtroom at various times simply because they have other business with the court.

15.23 Can I take a friend or family member with me to court?

Yes. Let your attorney know in advance if you intend to bring anyone to court with you. Some people important to you may be very emotional about your divorce or your spouse. Be sure to invite someone who is better able to focus attention on supporting you rather than on his or her own feelings.

15.24 Can my friends and family be present in the courtroom during my trial?

It depends upon whether they will be witnesses in your case. In most cases where witnesses other than you or your spouse are testifying, the attorneys request that the court *sequester* the witnesses. The judge would then order all witnesses, except you and your spouse, to leave the courtroom until after they have testified.

Once a witness has completed his or her testimony, he or she will ordinarily be allowed to remain in the courtroom for the remainder of the trial.

15.25 I want to do a great job testifying as a witness in my divorce trial. What are some tips?

Keep the following in mind to be a good witness on your own behalf:

- Tell the truth. Although this may not be always be comfortable, it is critical if you want your testimony to be believed by the judge. A witness' credibility is your most important asset.

- Listen carefully to the complete question before thinking of your answer. Wait to consider your answer until the full question is asked.

- Slow down. It's easy to speed up our speech when we are anxious or nervous. Taking your time with your answers ensures that the judge hears you and that the court reporter can accurately record your testimony.

- If you don't understand a question or don't know the answer, be sure to say so.

- If the question calls for a "yes" or "no" answer, simply say so. Then wait for the attorney to ask you the next question. If there is more you want to explain, remember that you have already told your attorney all the important facts and he or she will make sure you are allowed to give any testimony significant in your case.

- Don't argue with the judge or the lawyers.

- Take your time. You may be asked some questions that call for a thoughtful response. If you need a moment to reflect on an answer before you give it, allow yourself that time.

- Stop speaking if an objection is made by one of the lawyers. Wait until the judge has decided whether to allow you to answer.

- If you begin to feel emotional, your lawyer can ask for a short break.

15.26 Should I be worried about being cross-examined by my spouse's lawyer at trial?

If your case goes to trial, prepare to be asked some questions by your spouse's lawyer. Many of these questions will call for a simple "yes" or "no."

If you are worried about particular questions, discuss your concerns with your attorney. He or she can support you in giving a truthful response. Focus on preparing well for being asked questions by your spouse's lawyer. Try not to take the questions personally; remember that the lawyer is fulfilling a duty to advocate for your spouse's interests. Remember that you are just doing your best to tell the truth about the facts.

15.27 What happens on the day of trial?

Although no two trials are alike, the following steps will occur in most divorce trials:

- Attorneys meet with the judge in chambers to discuss procedural issues, such as how many witnesses will be called, how long the case will take to present, and when breaks might be taken.

- Attorneys give opening statements.

- Petitioner's attorney calls petitioner's witnesses to testify.

- Respondent's attorney may cross-examine each of them.

- Respondent's attorney calls respondent's witnesses to testify. Petitioner's attorney may cross-examine each of them.

- Petitioner's lawyer calls any *rebuttal witnesses,* that is, witnesses whose testimony contradicts the testimony of the respondent's witnesses.

- Closing arguments made first by the petitioner's attorney and then by the respondent's attorney.

15.28 Will the judge decide my case the day I go to court?

Possibly. Often there is so much information from the trial for the judge to consider that it is not possible for the judge to give an immediate ruling.

The judge may want to review documents, review the law, perform calculations, review his or her notes, and give thoughtful consideration to the issues to be decided. For this reason, it may be days, weeks, or in some cases, even longer before a ruling is made.

When a judge does not make a ruling immediately upon the conclusion of a trial, it is said that the case has been "taken under advisement."

16

The Appeals Process

You may find that despite your best efforts to settle your case, your divorce went to trial and the judge made major decisions that will have a serious impact on your future. You may be either gravely disappointed or even shocked by the judge's ruling.

The judge might have seen your case differently than you and your attorney did. Perhaps the judge made mistakes. Or it may be that Kansas law simply does not allow for the outcome you were hoping for.

Whatever the reasons for the court's rulings, you may feel that the judge's decisions are not ones which you can live with. If this is the case, talk to your lawyer immediately about your right to appeal. Together you can decide whether an appeal is in your best interest, or whether it is better to accept the court's ruling and invest your energy in moving forward with your future without an appeal.

16.1 How much time after my divorce do I have to file an appeal?

You must file an appeal within thirty days of the final order you wish to appeal. Because your attorney may also recommend filing one or more motions following your trial, and before you file an appeal, and the deadlines for such motions can be as short as fourteen days after the final order is received, discuss your options and your appeal rights with your lawyer as soon as you have received the judge's ruling.

A timely discussion with your attorney about your right to appeal is essential so important deadlines are not missed.

16.2   Can I appeal a temporary order?

No. Under Kansas law, only final orders may be appealed.

16.3   What parts of the decree can be appealed?

If you or your spouse is unhappy with final decisions made by the judge in your case, either of you can file an appeal. Decisions that can be appealed include custody, parenting time, child support, maintenance, division of property, and attorney's fees.

16.4   Will my attorney recommend I appeal specific aspects of the decree, or will I have to request it?

Your attorney may counsel you to file an appeal on certain issues of your case; you may also ask your lawyer whether there is a legitimate basis for an appeal of any decision you believe is wrong. Talk to your attorney regarding the decisions most dissatisfying to you. Your lawyer can advise which issues have the greatest likelihood of success on appeal, in light of the facts of your case and Kansas law.

16.5   When should an appeal be filed?

An appeal should be filed only after careful consultation with your lawyer when you believe that the judge has made a serious error under the law or the facts of your case. Among the factors you and your attorney should discuss are:

- Whether the judge had the authority under the law to make the decisions set forth in your decree
- The likelihood of the success of your appeal
- The risk that an appeal by you will encourage an appeal by your former spouse
- The cost of the appeal
- The length of time an appeal can be expected to take
- The impact of a delay in the case during the appeal

The deadline for filing an appeal is thirty days from the date that a final order is entered in your case. It is important that you are clear about the deadline that applies in your case, so talk to your attorney at once if you are thinking about an appeal.

16.6   Are there any disadvantages to filing an appeal?

There can be disadvantages to filing an appeal, including:

- Uncertainty as to the outcome
- Increased attorney's fees and costs
- The risks of a worse outcome on appeal than you received at trial
- Delay
- Prolonged conflict between you and your former spouse
- Risk of a second trial occurring after the appeal
- Difficulty in obtaining closure and moving forward with your life

16.7   Is an attorney necessary to appeal?

The appeals process is very detailed and specific, with set deadlines and specific court rules. Given the complex nature of the appellate process, you should have an attorney if you intend to file an appeal.

16.8   How long does the appeals process usually take?

It depends. An appeal can take anywhere from a year to over two years. An appeal may also result in the appellate court requiring further proceedings by the trial court. This will result in further expense and delay.

16.9   What are the steps in the appeals process?

There are many steps which your lawyer will take on your behalf in the appeal process, including:

- Identifying the issues to be appealed
- Filing a notice with the court of your intent to appeal
- Obtaining the necessary court documents and trial exhibits to send to the appellate court
- Obtaining transcript of trial, a written copy of testimony by witnesses and statements by the judge and the lawyers made in the presence of the court reporter

- Performing extensive legal research to support your arguments on appeal
- Preparing and filing a document known as a *brief,* which sets for the facts of the case and relevant law, complete with citations to the court transcript, court documents, and prior cases
- Making an oral argument before the judges of the appellate court

16.10 Is filing and pursuing an appeal expensive?

Yes. In addition to filing fees and lawyer fees, there is likely to be a substantial cost for the preparation of the transcript of the trial testimony. The cost of an appeal can sometimes exceed the cost of trial.

16.11 If I do not file an appeal, can I ever go back to court to change my decree?

Certain aspects of a decree are not modifiable, such as the division of property and debts or the award of attorney fees. Other parts of your decree, such as support or matters regarding the children, may be modified if there has been a "material and substantial change in circumstances."

A modification of custody or parenting time for minor children will also require you to show that the proposed change would be in their best interest.

If your decree did not provide for maintenance, it is unlikely that you will have any basis for a modification. Under Kansas law, court-awarded maintenance can only be modified under certain limited circumstances, and the awarded amount cannot typically be increased, only reduced. If you have questions about your divorce decree, consult with your attorney.

In Closing

As noted several times throughout our book, we hope you will feel more comfortable seeking out professional help to provide you with the resources to see you through this process. Hopefully this book has provided you with a framework for honest assessment of your situation.

At the end of your divorce, you will likely have mixed emotions. Acknowledge yourself for the courage you have shown in examining your unique situation, needs, and goals. Now, you are facing your future—recasting yourself into a new life. You are looking more closely at your living situation, the needs of your children, your financial security and your personal growth and healing. You are seeing your situation and telling the truth about what you now need. You are taking action to propel you into new possibilities.

From here, it is time to take inventory of the lessons learned, goals met, and action yet to take. Celebrate each of those steps forward and be gentle with yourself over the occasional misstep backward. You have transitioned through this time when everything is reduced to the core of you. Gone are the familiar habits of your marriage. With every day moving closer to the completion of your divorce, your grief will begin to subside and your energy improve as you move toward a fresh start.

No book can completely cover all of the likely questions you may have about your situation. This book cannot substitute for the customized advice you will get from an experienced attorney. We hope you will be empowered by this book to successfully close out one chapter of your life and begin the next.

Appendix

Sample Petition for Divorce

IN THE DISTRICT COURT OF_____COUNTY, KANSAS
CIVIL COURT DEPARTMENT

In the Matter of the Marriage of:)	
)	
**,)	Case No.
Petitioner,)	Court No.
and)	K.S.A. Chapters 23 and 60
)	
**,)	
Respondent.)	
_____)	

PETITION FOR DIVORCE

COMES NOW Petitioner, **, by and through counsel, and for his/her cause of action against the Respondent states and alleges as follows:

1. Petitioner is now and has been a bona fide resident of the State of Kansas for more than sixty (60) days preceding the filing of this action.

2. Respondent is a resident of _____County, Kansas with a correct address of _____.

3. The parties were married on the_____day of _____, in _____, and have been and are now husband and wife.

4. There are_____(_) children of this marriage, to-wit: **, born_____, _____, currently age_____, and **, born_____, _____, currently age_____, currently in the custody of Petitioner. Petitioner is not now pregnant.

199

Sample Petition for Divorce (Continued)

5. The parties have lived separate and apart since_____,_____.

6. The parties are fit and proper to be awarded the care, custody and control of the minor children. Pending the final determination of this cause, the primary residential custody of the parties' minor children should be with Petitioner, pursuant to Petitioner's Parenting Plan set forth in Petitioner's Motion for *Ex Parte* Temporary Orders.

7. Petitioner states:
   a. The children's present residence address is:_____.
   b. The children have not lived outside the State of Kansas during the five (5) years immediately preceding the filing of this petition.
   c. At all times during the five (5) years immediately preceding the filing of this Petition, the children have always resided with one or both of the parties to this action.
   d. Petitioner has not participated as party, witness, or in any other capacity in other litigation concerning the custody of the children in this or any other state.
   e. Petitioner has no information of any custody proceeding concerning the children in this or any other state.
   f. Petitioner knows of no person not a party to these proceedings who has physical custody of the children or who claims to have parenting time rights with respect to the minor children.

8. The parties are incompatible, one with the other, and because of this incompatibility Petitioner is entitled to a divorce from the Respondent on that ground.

9. The parties have accumulated certain property and debt over the period of their marriage which should be divided between them in an equitable fashion in light of all the facts and circumstances.

10. Petitioner requests that Petitioner be granted the following temporary orders as more thoroughly set forth in Petitioner's Motion for *Ex Parte* Temporary Orders:
    a. Child support for the minor children pursuant to the Kansas Child Support Guidelines; and
    b. Spousal maintenance in accordance with the _____ County Bench-Bar Family Law Guidelines; and
    c. Exclusive use and possession of the martial home located at: _____; and

Sample Petition for Divorce (Continued)

d. Exclusive use and possession of the vehicle currently in Petitioner's possession; and

e. An Order restraining the parties from altering, removing, selling, giving away, disposing, hiding, spending, mortgaging, pledging, or encumbering any marital assets, unless reasonably necessary for normal day-to-day business or personal expenses, for reasonable attorneys' fees and litigation expenses, in order to comply with this court's orders, or with written consent from both parties. Further, the Temporary Orders should restrain and prohibit either party from destroying, altering or hiding any personal or business records, whether written, electronic, or any other form and prohibited from modifying, altering, changing or canceling any coverage, persons insured or beneficiaries named on any existing insurance policy, whether for life, medical, dental, health, vehicle, disability, death, dismemberment or other type or kind of insurance, unless with written consent from both parties; and

f. An Order providing that the parties are restrained, unless agreed otherwise, as follows:

i. Neither party shall dispose, sell, mortgage, transfer, loan, hide, convert or sequester any of the marital assets of the parties.

ii. Neither party shall restrict access or remove the name of the other from any joint account or credit card.

iii. Neither party shall create any additional debt for which the other party may be liable.

iv. Neither party shall consume any of the marital assets of the parties, except to the extent necessary to pay normal household living expenses, marital debts due, taxes due on marital property, and reasonable costs of litigation.

v. Neither party shall change beneficiaries on any life, health, long- term care or disability insurance policies.

vi. Neither party shall change beneficiaries on any retirement plans and/or Individual Retirement Accounts.

vii. Neither party shall take loans against any retirement plans and or Individual Retirement Accounts.

viii. For joint legal custody pursuant to Petitioner's Proposed Parenting plan.

Sample Petition for Divorce (Continued)

ix. Neither party shall inflict or attempt to inflict any damages on the property of the other.

x. Neither party shall cancel any existing medical, dental or life insurance coverage(s) held by and/or for the benefit of the family.

xi. Neither party shall cancel any utility service.

xii. Each parent shall, **within thirty (30) days** of service of process of an Order for Parents Forever, attend (either separately or together) one co-parenting class on "Parenting Forever" conducted by _____County Domestic Court Services. The Parenting Forever class is held every Monday at 5:15 P.M. and every Wednesday at 8:15 A.M., except on holidays. Parenting Forever class is held at Domestic Court Services, _____. Parents should register on the day of the class no later than 15 minutes prior to the start time of the class and each parent must know and provide the teaching staff with their case number. Each parent shall pay his or her own $_____class fee within____**days** of the entry of this order. **Payment must be paid to the Court Trustee by cash or money order prior to attending the class.** All fee payments shall be paid to the District Court Trustee in person or by mail at _____.If payment is mailed, you must include your case number, return address and designate that this payment is for Parents Forever fees. Upon payment, the Trustee shall issue a receipt to the payor and enter the payment into the court file. All fees must be paid prior to any further hearing relating to the issues or finalization of this matter by order, decree or journal entry. Failure to pay the fee or failure to participate in good faith at Parents Forever may constitute Contempt of Court or could otherwise result in the Court assessing fines, attorney fees or other costs related to this order. Additional information may be obtained online at _____or by calling _____.

11 Neither party is now in the active military service of the United States, as defined by the Service Members Civil Relief Act of 2003, as amended, 50 U.S.C. §501.

Sample Petition for Divorce (Continued)

WHEREFORE, Petitioner, **, prays that upon final hearing she be granted by the Court a Decree of Divorce on the ground of incompatibility; that the marriage of the parties be dissolved; that the relief requested herein be granted; and the Court issue such other Orders as it deems just and equitable under the circumstances.

Respectfully Submitted:

_____

ATTORNEY NAME, KS#
ATTORNEY E-MAIL
ADDRESS
PHONE/ FAX
ATTORNEY FOR PETITIONER

_____

STATE OF KANSAS   )
) ss.
COUNTY OF_____)

**, of lawful age, being first duly sworn on oath, deposes and states:

That he/she is the Petitioner above-named; that he/she has read the above and foregoing Petition for Divorce, knows the contents thereof and that the facts, matters and statements contained therein are true and correct.

_____
_____, Petitioner

Subscribed and sworn to before me, the undersigned, a notary public in and for the county and state aforesaid, this_____day of _____,_____.

_____

Notary Public

My Commission Expires:

Sample Letter to the Respondent with Waiver of Service

manntuckermuir LLC
THE FAMILY LAW FIRM

(DATE)

Respondent's Name
Respondent's Address
Re: Case Caption
Dear Respondent:

    I represent your spouse, _____, in the above captioned divorce matter that was filed in the _____County District Court on _____. Enclosed please find the following file- stamped pleadings:

    1. Petition for Divorce; and

    2. Child Support Worksheet; and

    3. Motion for *Ex Parte* Temporary Orders; and

    4. Domestic Relations Affidavit of Petitioner.

    Also enclosed is a Waiver of Service and Entry of Appearance. My client has requested that, rather than having you served by law enforcement or some other person authorized to serve process, that we simply send the paperwork to you. You need to review the Waiver of Service and Entry of Appearance and then, if you choose to accept service of the documents in this fashion, sign the Waiver in the presence of a notary public and have the document notarized. You may fax, scan and e-mail, or mail the Waiver back to me. I've enclosed a self-addressed stamped envelope for your return of the original Waiver, which I must receive back from you.

    We ask that you please return the signed, notarized Waiver to our office in the enclosed self- addressed stamped envelope within seven (7) days of the date of this letter. Should our office not receive the Waiver of Service within seven days of the date of this letter, we will request formal service through the Court.

Sincerely,

Attorney

CC: Client (email only)
Enclosures

Sample Entry of Appearance
and Waiver of Notice and Service

IN THE DISTRICT COURT OF_____COUNTY,
KANSAS CIVIL COURT DEPARTMENT

In the Matter of the Marriage of:	)	
**,	)	Case No.
Petitioner,	)	Court No.
and	)	K.S.A. Chapters 23 and 60
	)	
**,	)	
Respondent.	)	
_____	)	

ENTRY OF APPEARANCE AND WAIVER OF NOTICE & SERVICE

COMES NOW the Respondent, and acknowledges that he/she has received a copy of the Petition for Divorce, Child Support Worksheet, Motion for Ex Parte Temporary Orders, *Ex Parte* Temporary Orders, and Domestic Relations Affidavit of Petitioner. The Respondent voluntarily enters his/her appearance, waiving personal service of process upon him/her, and further consents that the Petition may be heard by the Court. I understand that I have twenty one (21) days from today to answer or otherwise respond to the Petition, or I may be found in default.

_____

_____, Respondent

STATE OF_____)_____)
)ss:
COUNTY OF_____)

_____, Respondent, of lawful age, being first duly sworn on oath, states that he/she is the person above named; that he/she has read the above and foregoing Entry of Appearance and Waiver of Notice & Service; knows the contents thereof and that the facts and matters therein contained are true and correct.

_____

_____, Respondent

Subscribed and sworn to before me this_____day of _____, 2016.
My appointment expires:

_____

NOTARY PUBLIC

Resources

Annual Credit Report Request Service

www.annualcreditreport.com
P.O. Box 105283
Atlanta, GA 30348-5283
(877) 322–8228

This website offers a centralized service for consumers to request annual credit reports. It was created by the three nationwide consumer credit reporting companies, Equifax, Experian, and TransUnion. AnnualCreditReport.com processes requests for free credit file disclosures (commonly called credit reports). Under the *Fair and Accurate Credit Transactions Act (FACT Act),* consumers can request and obtain a free credit report once every twelve months from each of the three nationwide consumer credit reporting companies. AnnualCreditReport.com offers consumers a fast and convenient way to request, view and print their credit reports in a secure Internet environment. It also provides options to request reports by telephone and by mail.

Internal Revenue Service (IRS)

www.irs.gov

Phone: (800) 829-1040 tax assistance for individual tax questions or (800) 829-4933 for business tax questions.

The IRS web site allows you to search for any key word, review publications and information on tax questions, or submit a question via e-mail or phone to an IRS representative.

Kansas Child Support Payment Center
www.kspaycenter.com
(877) 572-5722
This site includes specific sections for individuals receiving support, individuals paying support, and for employers of individuals paying support. A toll-free automated system to check on the status of the receipt and disbursement of child support, as well as any outstanding balance owed, can be accessed by calling (877) 631-9973.

Kansas Department for Children and Families
Child Support Services
www.dcf.ks.gov/services/CSS/Pages/default.aspx
Phone: (888) 757-2445
The Child Support Services and Enforcement Program helps children obtain financial support from both parents, enables current public assistance recipients to end their reliance on welfare, and can help prevent single parents from entering public assistance.

Kansas Legal Services
www.kansaslegalservices.org
Phone toll-free: (800) 723-6953
The mission of Kansas Legal Services is to provide quality civil legal services for those who have nowhere else to turn. Legal Services provides referral, advice, brief service and placement for extended representation with local offices across the state.

National Domestic Violence Hotline
(800) 799-7233
www.thehotline.org

Social Security Administration
www.ssa.gov
Office of Public Inquiries
Windsor Park Building
6401 Security Boulevard
Baltimore, MD 21235
(800) 772-1213
The website enables users to search for a question or word, submit questions via e-mail, or review recent publications.

Other Recommended Websites
www.huffingtonpost.com/divorce
www.uptoparents.org

Glossary

Affidavit: A written statement of facts made under oath and signed before a notary public. Affidavits are used primarily when there will not be a hearing in open court with live testimony. The attorney will prepare an affidavit to present relevant facts. Affidavits may be signed by the parties or in some cases by witnesses. The person signing the affidavit may be referred to as the *affiant*.

Allegation: A statement that one party claims is true.

Alimony: Court-ordered spousal support payments from one party to another, often to enable the recipient spouse to become economically independent. In Kansas, this is called *maintenance.*

Answer: A written response to the petition for divorce. It serves to admit or deny the allegations in the complaint and may also make claims against the opposing party. This is sometimes called a *responsive pleading.* An answer should be filed within twenty-one days of either (a) the petition being served by the sheriff or (b) the defendant's voluntary appearance being filed with the court.

Appeal: The process by which a higher court reviews the decision of a lower court. In Kansas family law cases, a person will first file an appeal with the Kansas Court of Appeals. After that appeal is decided there may be a further appeal to the Kansas Supreme Court.

Application to modify: A party's written request to the court to change a prior order regarding custody, child support, alimony or any other order that the court may change by law. Sometimes also referred to as a *motion.*

Application for relocation: A parent's written request to the court seeking permission to relocate to another state with the children.

Child support: Financial support for a child paid by the noncustodial parent to the custodial parent.

Court order: A court-issued document setting forth the judge's orders. An order can be issued based upon the parties' agreement or the judge's decision. An order may require the parties to perform certain acts or set forth their rights and responsibilities. An order is put in writing, signed by the judge, and filed with the court.

Court order acceptable for processing (COAP): A type of court order that provides for payment of civil service retirement to a former spouse.

Contempt of court: The willful and intentional failure of a party to comply with a court order, judgment, or decree. Contempt may be punishable by a fine or jail.

Contested case: Any case in which the parties cannot reach an agreement. A contested case will result in a trial to have the judge decide disputed issues.

Cross-examination: The questioning of a witness by the opposing counsel during trial or at a deposition, in response to questions asked by the other lawyer.

Custody: The legal right and responsibility awarded by a court for the possession of, care of, and decision-making for a minor child.

Decree of divorce: A final court order dissolving the marriage, dividing property and debts, ordering support, and entering other orders regarding finances and the minor children.

Deposition: A witness's testimony taken out of court, under oath, and in the presence of lawyers and a court reporter. If a person gives a different testimony at the time of trial, he or she can be impeached with the deposition testimony; that is, statements made at a deposition can be used to show untruthfulness if a different answer is given at trial.

Direct examination: The initial questioning of a witness in court by the lawyer who called him or her to the stand.

Discovery: A process used by attorneys to discover information from the opposing party for the purpose of fully assessing a case for settlement or trial. Types of discovery include interrogatories, requests for production of documents, and requests for admissions.

Dissolution: The act of terminating or dissolving a marriage.

Equitable distribution of property: The method by which real and personal property and debts are divided in a divorce. Given all economic circumstances of the parties, Kansas law requires that marital property and debts be divided in a fair and reasonable manner.

Ex parte: Usually in reference to a motion, the term used to describe an appearance of only one party before the judge, without other party being present. For example, an *ex parte* restraining order may be granted immediately after the filing of a petition for divorce.

Guardian *ad litem* (GAL): A person, often a lawyer or mental health professional, appointed by court to conduct an investigation regarding the children's best interest.

Hearing: Any proceeding before the court for the purpose of resolving disputed issues between the parties through presentation of testimony, affidavits, exhibits, or argument.

Hold-harmless clause: A term in a court order that requires one party to assume responsibility for a debt and to protect the other spouse from any loss or expense in connection with it, as in "to hold harmless from liability."

Interrogatories: Written questions sent from one party to the other that are used to obtain facts or opinions related to the divorce.

Joint custody: The shared right and responsibility of both parents awarded by the court for possession, care, and decision-making for children.

Mediation: A process by which a neutral third party facilitates negotiations between the parties on a wide range of issues.

Motion: A written application or request to the court for relief, such as temporary child support, custody, or restraining orders.

No-fault divorce: The type of divorce Kansas has that court does not require evidence of marital misconduct. This means that abandonment, cruelty, and adultery are neither relevant nor required to be proven for the purposes of granting the divorce.

Notice of hearing: A written statement sent to the opposing lawyer or spouse listing the date and place of a hearing and the nature of the matters that will be heard by the court. In Kansas, one party is required to give the other party reasonable notice of any court hearing.

Party: The person in a legal action whose rights or interests will be affected by the divorce. For example, in a divorce the parties include the wife and husband.

Pending: During the case. For example, the judge may award you temporary support while your case is pending.

Petition: The first document filed with the clerk of the court in an action for divorce, separation, or paternity. The petition sets forth the facts on which the requested relief is based.

Petitioner: The person who files the petition initiating a divorce.

Pleadings: Documents filed with the court seeking a court order.

Qualified domestic relations order (QDRO): A type of court order that provides for direct payment from a retirement account to a former spouse.

Qualified medical support order (QMSO): A type of court order that provides a former spouse certain rights regarding medical insurance and information.

Request for production of documents: A written request for documents sent from one party to the other during the discovery process.

Respondent: The responding party to a divorce; the party who did not file the petition initiating the divorce.

Sequester: To order prospective witnesses out of the courtroom until they have concluded giving their testimony.

Setoff: A debt or financial obligation of one spouse that is deducted from the debt or financial obligation of the other spouse.

Settlement: The agreed resolution of disputed issues.

Show cause: Written application to the court to hold another person in contempt of court for violating or failing to comply with a current court order.

Stipulation: An agreement reached between parties or an agreement by their attorneys.

Subpoena: A document delivered to a person or witness that requires him or her to appear in court, appear for a deposition, or produce documents. Failure to comply could result in punishment by the court. A subpoena requesting documents is called a *subpoena duces tecum*.

Temporary restraining order (TRO): An order of the court prohibiting a party from certain behavior. For example, a temporary restraining order may order a person not to transfer any funds during a pending divorce action.

Trial: A formal court hearing in which the judge will decide disputed issues raised by the parties' pleadings.

Under advisement: A term used to describe the status of a case, usually after a court hearing on a motion or a trial, when the judge has not yet made a decision.

Index

Index

217

W

About the Authors

Scott M. Mann is a founding member of MannTuckerMuir, LLC, The Family Law Firm. His practice is focused exclusively on family law issues, including divorce, determination of parentage (paternity), spousal support, child custody, and child support. Scott also handles post-decree matters such as modification of support, modification of custody and parenting time, and enforcement of support and custody orders and agreements.

Scott handles complex cases throughout the Kansas City metropolitan area. His practice includes mediation, collaborative divorce, and traditional litigation of family law cases. He is a graduate of the University of Missouri at Columbia School of Law. He is licensed to practice law in both Missouri and Kansas. Scott is a fellow of the American Academy of Matrimonial Lawyers and of the International Academy of Family Lawyers. He is a past president of the Family Law Section of the Kansas Bar Association. He frequently teaches a variety of family law topics to other attorneys.

Scott has served as editor for several state and national family law publications. He also serves as the editor of the *Practitioner's Guide to Kansas Family Law* (Kansas Bar Assn., 2d. Ed. 2013). He is a founding member of the Collaborative Divorce Professionals of Greater Kansas City. Scott has also been frequently named to the following peer-rated lists: *U.S. News* Best Lawyer in Family Law, *Kansas City Business Journal* Best of the Bar, and Super Lawyers of Missouri and Kansas. He may be contacted through his website at: **www.manntuckermuir.com.**

Stephanie Tucker Muir is a founding member of MannTuckerMuir, LLC. Her practice is dedicated exclusively to family law—divorce, determination of parentage (paternity), spousal support, child custody, and child support. Because a client's issues and legal needs, particularly with young children, may not end with a decree of divorce, Stephanie also handles post-decree matters such as modification of support, modification of custody and parenting time, and enforcement of support and custody orders and agreements.

Stephanie received her Juris Doctor degree as well as her undergraduate degree from the University of Kansas. She is a fellow of the American Academy of Matrimonial Lawyers, a Kansas family law mediator, and a member of the Kansas Bar Association; she is also a member of the Johnson County Bar Association and the Missouri Bar Association. She is a founding barrister and an officer of the executive committee for the Johnson County Family Law American Inns of Court. She was selected as a Super Lawyer by *Super Lawyers* magazine. Stephanie is licensed in both Kansas and Missouri.

It is always Stephanie's goal not only to provide solid legal representation but also to be compassionate with her clients during some of the most difficult times of their lives. She may contacted through her website at: **www.manntuckermuir.com.**

Divorce Titles from Addicus Books

Visit our online catalog at www.AddicusBooks.com

Divorce in Alabama: The Legal Process, Your Rights, and What to Expect $21.95

Divorce in Arizona: The Legal Process, Your Rights, and What to Expect. $21.95

Divorce in California: The Legal Process, Your Rights, and What to Expect $21.95

Divorce in Connecticut: The Legal Process, Your Rights, and What to Expect $21.95

Divorce in Florida: The Legal Process, Your Rights, and What to Expect $21.95

Divorce in Georgia: Simple Answers to Your Legal Questions $21.95

Divorce in Hawaii: The Legal Process, Your Rights, and What to Expect $21.95

Divorce in Illinois: The Legal Process, Your Rights, and What to Expect $21.95

Divorce in Kansas: The Legal Process, Your Rights, and What to Expect $21.95

Divorce in Louisiana: The Legal Process, Your Rights, and What to Expect $21.95

Divorce in Maine: The Legal Process, Your Rights, and What to Expect $21.95

Divorce in Maryland: The Legal Process, Your Rights, and What to Expect $21.95

Divorce in Michigan: The Legal Process, Your Rights, and What to Expect. $21.95

Divorce in Mississippi: The Legal Process, Your Rights, and What to Expect. $21.95

A Guide to Divorce in Missouri: Simple Answers to Complex Questions $21.95

Divorce in Nebraska: The Legal Process, Your Rights, and What to Expect—2nd Edition $21.95

Divorce in Nevada: The Legal Process, Your Rights, and What to Expect. $21.95

Divorce in New Jersey: The Legal Process, Your Rights, and What to Expect $21.95

Divorce in New York: The Legal Process, Your Rights, and What to Expect $21.95

Divorce in North Carolina: Answers to Your Legal Questions. $21.95

Divorce in Oklahoma: The Legal Process, Your Rights, and What to Expect $21.95

Divorce in Tennessee: The Legal Process, Your Rights, and What to Expect $21.95

Divorce in Virginia: The Legal Process, Your Rights, and What to Expect $21.95

Divorce in Washington: The Legal Process, Your Rights, and What to Expect $21.95

Divorce in West Virginia: The Legal Process, Your Rights, and What to Expect $21.95

Divorce in Wisconsin: The Legal Process, Your Rights, and What to Expect $21.95

Daily Meditations for Healing from Divorce: Discovering the New You. $21.95

To Order Books:
Visit us online at: www.AddicusBooks.com
Call toll free: (800) 888-4741

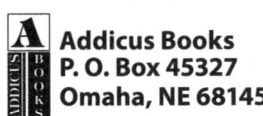

Addicus Books
P. O. Box 45327
Omaha, NE 68145

To order books from Addicus Books:

Please send:

_____copies of_____
                                    (Title of book)

      at $ _____each   TOTAL _____
      NE residents add 5% sales tax   _____

      Add Shipping/Handling
          $6.75 for first book
          $1.10 for each additional book _____

           TOTAL ENCLOSED   _____

Name _____
Address _____
City _____State_____Zip _____

     ☐ Visa   ☐ Mastercard   ☐ AMEX   ☐ Discover
Credit card number _____
Expiration date _____
Three digit CVV number on back of card _____

Order by credit card or personal check.

To Order Books:
Visit us online at: www.AddicusBooks.com
Call toll free: (800) 888-4741

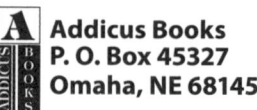

Addicus Books
P. O. Box 45327
Omaha, NE 68145

Scott Bill payment

- very much need your services
- ~~very pleased to be c you~~
  ~~How can we make this work~~
- In order to make this work
  need a plan that's
  [Sustainable]

- I am not able to move
  forward @ this $ rate
  considering [options.]
  - not good time to go into debt
  [$tress] of $ not good either

Can you attempt to project cost?
Length of time Based on experience
so I can plan $